Weaving a Just Future for Children

D1283476

Many Blessings,
Lynne

Weaving a Just Future for Children

An Advocacy Guide

Diane C. Olson

DIANE C. OLSON

LAURA DEAN F. FRIEDRICH

Laura Dean F. Friedrich

With hope for all children!

DISCIPLESHIP RESOURCES

P O BOX 340003 • NASHVILLE, TN 37203-0003
www.discipleshipresources.org

Library of Congress Cataloging-in-Publication Data

Olson, Diane C.
  Weaving a just future for children : an advocacy guide / Diane C.
Olson, Laura Dean F. Friedrich.
    p. cm.
  Includes bibliographical references.
  ISBN 978-0-88177-547-1
  1. Church work with children. 2. Child welfare. 3. Children's
rights. 4. Child abuse—Religious aspects—Christianity. I. Friedrich,
Laura Dean Ford. II. Title.
  BV639.C4O47 2008
  270.8'3083—dc22
                                    2008029623

Scripture quotations, unless otherwise indicated, are from the New Revised Standard Version of the Bible, copyright © 1989 by the Division of Christian Education of the National Council of the Churches of Christ in the USA. All rights reserved. Used by Permission.

Original pen and ink art by Jim Osborn Illustration

Acknowledgments

EVERY BOOK IS WRITTEN through the efforts and influences of many people. We are grateful to several people at the General Board of Discipleship and Discipleship Resources:

- Mary Alice Gran, who first affirmed our call to write this book,
- George Donigian, our "first" editor, who worked with us for a year in the writing process, and
- Terrie Livaudais, our copy editor, who was collaborative and kind as the book became real.

We both thank Angela Olson Kalthoff for her photograph of the authors.

We greatly appreciate the support of our bishops: Bishop Sally Dyck (Resident Bishop Minnesota Area Conference) and Bishop Hee-Soo Jung (Resident Bishop Northern Illinois Area Conference) and all of our bishops' work on behalf of children.

We each had our own cheering sections as the work progressed:

Diane gives thanks for:

- the children who helped her understand their world, especially David, Emily, and Amanda, and the children of the churches she has served;
- friends and family who supported and encouraged her, especially Rev. Deb Walkes and the people of Fridley United Methodist Church; and
- Laura Dean, who was very patient with Diane's long sentences and rambling paragraphs.

Laura Dean gives thanks for:

- the parents who trusted her with their children and taught her about children and parenting, especially Michal and Ron and the families of Casa Central and ChildServ;
- friends and family who supported and encouraged her, especially Corydon, Elizabeth, Laura Ford, and the people of Holy Covenant United Methodist Church; and
- Diane, who first conceived the idea and then convinced Laura Dean that she could be a part of it.

And we both thank God for God's abundant grace and hope for the future for children.

We dedicate this book to
All Children
and
those who advocate for them.

Contents

Part III—The Weft: Discipleship and Vocation

Study Guide

Appendixes

Foreword

ADVOCACY IS WHAT a parent does without a second thought when one's own child is in need. What comes less naturally to us is to advocate for the well-being of others' children and yet that's what caring for the "least of these" requires. I wear a button that says, "So, how are the children?" One day I had it on when I went to catch a flight at the airport. The woman checking me in saw it and responded, "My children are doing just fine, thanks!" I told her I was glad that her children were doing fine, but we all need to make sure that all children are doing "just fine."

Are we doing what we have been called to do for the children? For all the children, not just our own? Even when there is a *will* for advocacy, churches do not always know *how* to do it in an effective manner consistent with our Christian values. This book will help us learn how to make sure that neither the government nor the church is shirking its responsibility for the children.

The Jewish philosopher, mystic, and prophet, Abraham Joshua Heschel, of the 20th century, once stated:

> For many of us the march from Selma to Montgomery was both protest and prayer. Legs are not lips, and walking is not kneeling. And yet our legs uttered songs. Even without words, our march was worship. I felt my legs were praying.[1]

Heschel is known for revitalizing a worshipful attitude toward God within Judaism as well as advocating for justice. He prayed and he acted. He worshiped and he advocated. His legs and his lips were used for both.

Weaving a Just Future for All Children: An Advocacy Guide renews our biblical challenge to be advocates for the most vulnerable in all society—the children. One of the United Methodist Council of Bishops'

Vision Pathways to fulfill the mission of The United Methodist Church—to make disciples of Jesus Christ for the transformation of the world—is to reach and transform the lives of new generations of children. We are called to be advocates for children's spiritual and physical lives; their well-being has been entrusted to us.

This book comes as a reminder to some and a challenge to others that as Christians we are called to care for the children who are the "least of these" in our midst, including care that can only come through our state and federal budgets. In Minnesota, Children's Sabbath celebrations are regularly practiced in many United Methodist churches. A Christian educator reported that a Children's Sabbath was considered by some as being "too anti-government," implying that the government is not doing what it is entrusted to do for the care of the children.

No one would intentionally work against the well-being of children, would they? Yet daily decisions are made by our state and federal governments that balance budgets on the backs of children even while promising that no child is left behind. An advocate is someone who speaks for another, calls for aid, or gives help on behalf of one who cannot speak or even ask for help. Children cannot speak or advocate for themselves in legislative halls.

Children need advocacy in order to ensure that "all the children are above average" (to quote Garrison Keillor's popular phrase).[2] It takes a lot of vigilance to help state and federal legislators do the right thing for children. As long as no one is watching, speaking, rallying, and pressuring, it is easy to overlook those who don't have a voice or vote. Advocacy is using our lips and legs to help someone else; it's walking and praying, protesting and worshiping.

Bishop Sally Dyck
Minnesota Annual Conference, The United Methodist Church

Foreword Notes

1. Reuven Kimelman, "Abraham Joshua Heschel: Our Generation's Teacher," www.crosscurrents.org/heschel.htm
2. Used by permission, Garrison Keillor.

Foreword

CHURCH LEADERS—lay and clergy—have identified four themes as the primary emphasis for United Methodists to guide the vision for the Church in the 21st century. These four mission initiatives include:

- Leadership development
- Building new congregations and revitalizing existing ones
- Ministry with the poor, particularly children
- Combating the preventable diseases cultivated by poverty, such as malaria, HIV/AIDS, and tuberculosis

At first look, persons who care about children might be relieved to see that children "made the list." A second, more thoughtful review tells us that children are at the heart of all four of these mission initiatives. The future of our denomination depends on how well we understand that reality and how effectively we carry out the work given to us by Christ when he called his disciples to ministries with the least, the last, and the lost.

One of the important responsibilities of a bishop in The United Methodist Church is that of teaching the faithful in matters of faith and discipleship. I commend *Weaving a Just Future for All Children* to individuals and congregations across the denomination. It points out in clear language and practical examples that child advocacy is as integral to discipleship as worship and education. Diane and Laura Dean have given us in the church an excellent tool for integrating advocacy into our ministries with and on behalf of children, particularly children who live in poverty.

The second chapter of Luke contains four extraordinary stories that contain important information about Jesus' childhood. Embedded in these stories, we find a number of the critical ingredients that contribute to positive growth and development in a child: committed parents (Mary and Joseph) who nurtured and cared for him; ordinary, working people (shepherds) who celebrated his birth; religious persons (Simeon and Anna) who gave thanks for this special child; and learned teachers who listened to Jesus at age 12 and heard God speaking to them. Verse 40 tells us, "And the child grew and became strong, filled with wisdom; and the favor of God was upon him." The child is Jesus, a child like none other. And yet, is not this description of the young Jesus what we want for all children, in all places?

Yes! We want all children to grow up healthy, gain physical and emotional strength, increase intellectual capacity, and receive a spiritual life fed by God's presence and power. We make this declaration with conviction, while, at the same time, we know that many children will encounter significant barriers in their lives more often than abundant blessings. God hears the cries of these children, the Ishmaels of our communities and our world, and God calls people of faith—you and me—to advocate for these vulnerable ones, the children in our midst marginalized by poverty, prejudice, racism, and injustice.

Weaving a Just Future for All Children gives all of us who are disciples of Jesus Christ a place to begin. We have much to learn, and Diane and Laura Dean have written an important book to guide our individual and corporate advocacy for children, youth, and their families. Open your hearts and minds to new possibilities of ministry through advocacy. Listen and hear God speak to you through your reading and reflections. Advocacy for children should infuse all that we are and do in Christ's name. "I am about to do a new thing; now it springs forth, do you not perceive it? I will make a way in the wilderness and rivers in the desert." (Isaiah 43:19)

Bishop Hee-Soo Jung
Northern Illinois Annual Conference,
The United Methodist Church

Introduction

WE GREET YOU—our readers—with a great sense of gratitude and hope. You hold in your hands the results of our prayers and planning, writing and revising, and we feel humbled and blessed by your interest and confidence. We give thanks for the opportunity to share some of our experiences and insights with you and invite you to a new and renewed commitment on behalf of God's children in all places. We welcome you to the discipline and practice of child advocacy!

Four images of Jesus' life and ministry have nourished our work: welcoming, blessing, reaching out, and receiving. Jesus talked with the disciples about greatness by bringing a child into the circle and saying, "Whoever welcomes one such child in my name welcomes me." (Matthew 18:15) He responded to the disciples' efforts to keep children away by blessing them and their parents. "And he took them up in his arms, laid his hands on them, and blessed them." (Mark 10:16) Another time Jesus stopped what he was doing and reached out to a child who was in great distress. "Then he . . . took the child's father and mother and those who were with him, and went in where the child was." (Mark 5:40c) Finally, Jesus received the gift of a child and fed a lot of hungry people. "Then Jesus took the loaves, and when he had given thanks, he distributed them to those who were seated; so also with the fish, as much as they wanted." (John 6:11) Woven together these images describe the basic premise of this book: taking action on behalf of and with children is child advocacy, and advocacy comes in many forms and encompasses a wide variety of actions.

Have you ever . . .

- Taught an adult education class on children's issues?
- Volunteered to tutor a child or teen-ager in reading or math?

- Talked with a legislator about public school funding?
- Participated in a public witness on behalf of children?

If you have done any of these things, you are a child advocate! And since you are a child advocate, we have written *Weaving a Just Future for All Children* to assist you and other Christian disciples to recognize advocacy as an integral aspect of your ministry with and for children and youth.

As you begin reading, we encourage you to invite other church leaders to join you in this important endeavor. We have written this advocacy guide with a number of people in mind:

- Clergy
- Christian educators
- Children's and youth ministers
- Laity—leaders and volunteers in local churches
- Persons in ministry in the world (lay and clergy who work in both secular and faith-based organizations)
- Congregational committees, women's groups, and men's groups
- Seminary faculty and students

Advocacy is as integral to discipleship as prayer and worship.

People of good will just like you—people who care deeply about the well-being of children and youth—fill our churches. All across the country, our congregations strive to implement faithful ministries that support, nurture, and guide these young people, both within the church and in the wider community. In recent years, our United Methodist churches have responded to the Bishops' call to an Initiative on Children and Poverty, supported Hope for the Children of Africa, and developed Safe Sanctuary policies and procedures to ensure the health and safety of children in our churches. In addition, many of our local churches operate or support food pantries; carry out community-based midweek children's programs; provide tutoring for school-age children; operate early care and education for children under the age of six; as well a variety of activities for children and youth of all ages.

As persons of faith, we often realize that these efforts, although commendable, do not address the full range of problems faced by the children, youth, and parents in our care. Church members want to do more, but they are often overwhelmed by the complexity of the problems of the children they know and the many others they do not know. They recognize that their commitment to Christ—their discipleship—requires more than acts of mercy, but they do not always know how to get to the root causes of the myriad of issues that confront children, youth, parents, and guardians in their congregations and communities.

The missing link is advocacy. *Advocacy* is not a word heard frequently in our local churches. Yet advocacy—speaking, intervening, standing for, organizing, witnessing—is the vehicle for connecting the pastoral and prophetic mandates of the Christian faith. Christ calls his modern-day disciples to do acts of kindness and, at the same time, work for justice, all in deep spiritual relationship with God. For United Methodists, our Wesleyan heritage inspires and our Social Principles demand these greater efforts on behalf of all children and youth, but especially for those who are vulnerable, in pain, alone, lost. Advocacy is as integral to discipleship as prayer and worship.

Therefore, we invite you and other disciples from all levels of the church to take on a broader understanding of advocacy as a new or renewed component of your commitment to Christ and your witness to the world. This guide will inform and strengthen you for this journey by:

1. Articulating the biblical and theological framework for advocacy as a legitimate focus of ministry within and by the local church;
2. Enabling local churches, groups, or individuals to hear the concerns of children and their families and to understand their perspectives;

3. Helping local churches and individuals to strengthen and expand their advocacy efforts (ministries); and

4. Empowering local churches to integrate advocacy into all aspects of the congregation's mission and ministry.

This advocacy guide is a powerful tool for all who care about children. Through stories, Scriptures, statistics, strategies, and you will hear the concerns of children and their families and gain conviction and skill for advocating on their behalf. We have organized this book into three sections according to the process of weaving. In weaving we begin with a loom, the structure with which weaving is done. The vertical threads are called the warp, and the side to side threads are known as the weft. Adding the weft to the warp on the loom creates a new fabric.

Part I—The Loom: Biblical and Contemporary Stories

In the opening section of the book, we discuss the biblical and historical imperatives for caring and acting for children. We articulate a theological framework for advocacy as a ministry of the local church and remind readers of our Wesleyan heritage to visit, care for, and teach children. We conclude this first section with an overview of the world of children.

Part II—The Warp: Practices, Issues, and Tools

Through chapters 4–7, we will present the different models and venues of advocacy. We point out a number of the critical issues that affect the lives of children (e.g., safety, health care, education) and we present practical ways of "doing" advocacy in church and community settings. We also suggest a variety of data sources, tools, and strategies to undergird your important work, your ministry, of acting for children.

Part III—The Weft: Discipleship and Vocation

In the third section, we encourage disciples and congregations to consider the church's role in public policy matters, and we discuss the important ways parents, grandparents, and guardians engage in advocacy. The final chapter defines advocacy as vocation and an essential element of our involvement in the reign of God, the beloved community.

We have written the book with both individuals and groups in mind. We hope that you will encourage others in your church to read and study *Weaving a Just Future for All Children* together in your covenant group, mission committee, Church Council, or women's group. You will find thought-provoking reflection questions at the end of each chapter, practical steps for those who want to enhance their learning through experience and action, and a group study guide at the end of the book. We have also included valuable resources and references in the appendixes, including annotated bibliography, advocacy organizations and websites, and public policy tools. Finally, we have woven Scripture, tradition, experience, and theology into a reader-friendly and usable text. Most of our stories come from our own experience. Where the stories belong to others, we have noted that and obtained permission for their use. In every case we have disguised names and other facts to protect identities. Given these changes to original stories, we still know them all to be true.

We have attempted to present a balance between increasing knowledge and building capacity through examples, tools, and resources. It is our great hope that our ideas and suggestions will be helpful for people of faith in a wide range of situations and experiences. We confess that we have written with a cultural perspective and experience largely shaped by the realities of living in the United States of America. Our experience in the global community is limited, but our hearts care deeply for the children and youth who live, some in extremely difficult circumstances, in all parts of the world. We pray that our sisters and brothers who live and minister in the far reaches of the United Methodist connection, as well as in our ecumenical community, will find some useful application for their children, congregations, and communities.

Our advocacy guide demonstrates that advocacy is embedded in our discipleship rather than being something separate, to be carried out by a few persons in the secular arena. Therefore it is our goal to engage the church community and individual disciples in witnessing for children and organizing acts of mercy, love, and justice on their behalf—all in the context of living one's faith in the world.

We believe that *Weaving a Just Future for Children* will make a lasting, positive impact on the lives of children and youth as together, we learn to weave advocacy through all our pastoral, prophetic, and discipleship ministries.

Our prayers and hopes are with you all.

PART I: THE LOOM

Biblical and Contemporary Stories

CHAPTER 1

Seeing Children through God's Eyes

⟨ The Frame for Weaving ⟩

Story

One of the most precious memories a woman can describe is being mother to a nursing baby in the early morning hours. Like every mother, Diane has vivid memories of the sweet morning joy of each of her children, their baby softness, their tiny hands curled around her fingers or lying softly on her breast. She cradled their small forms in the crook of her arm while they nursed frantically at first, then more slowly as they felt the satisfaction of a filling tummy. She remembers the cries and struggles of their physical and emotional needs. As she thinks about those experiences, Diane also recognizes the fiercely protective love she felt for them. She realized that she was the only human they had in those moments, and the only one they needed.

Theological Framework

Theology is God (*theo*) study (*logy*). Theology, then, is thinking about the nature of God and defining ourselves in relation to God. Images help us in this process. Naming the various images that bring God to mind helps all of us understand something about the nature of God. The Bible contains many images for and understandings of God, including a mother hen, a still small voice, and a loving father. In the story above, God is like a nursing mother cradling an infant.

Diane's feelings provide a basis for understanding God's love for children, those who need to be protected, nourished, loved, and valued for whom they are in this moment. God must love children very much to have created humanity in this relational and interdependent way. Thinking about God's love for children is theology, and this chapter summarizes a framework for considering a theology of children.[1]

At times in the church's history, theology has been a scary word, reserved for deep thinkers called "theologians" who often resided in stone-walled isolated buildings and had limited knowledge of the world outside. In more recent years, individuals with advanced degrees, numerous publications, and important positions in prestigious universities and seminaries have been recognized as the theologians. The authors of this book believe that the "work" of theology belongs to everyone, including biblical scholars, national experts, lay speakers, local church preachers, and the average person in the pew, along with children and youth! Theology—our efforts to understand the nature of God and the relationship we have with God—is an integral part of each modern-day disciple's everyday life. The Bible, in concert with our reason (knowledge), tradition (history), and experience, inform our God study, our theology, and our efforts to understand God.[2]

Perhaps you are wondering why a book on advocacy for children starts with a chapter on theology. The introduction of this book presents a working definition of advocacy as "taking action on behalf of children." That definition will expand in the chapters that follow, but taking action on behalf of children is at the heart of it. The basic questions for this chapter are, then, what is the relationship between your understanding of God and your concern for children? What do experience and knowledge tell you about what God might think about children? How does your understanding of the nature of God, particularly related to children, lead you to take action on behalf of children?

This chapter will help you explore these questions by discussing several important concepts—the nature of God, being created in the image of God, the incarnation of God, and God's call to justice. By thinking about your own answers to these questions, you begin to create a loom or frame upon which your advocacy for children will be woven. Theology provides the support and structure for the weaving of your advocacy vocation, your call to advocacy ministries inside and outside of the church.

The Nature of God

The authenticity of children's faith helps all people understand God's love better. Diane has served as a Christian educator at a midsize church and remembers one such experience early in her ministry. It was one of those very hard days for all church leaders, shortly before Christmas with many activities and programs. That particular Sunday morning was not going well. The pastor had reminded her that she was late with her monthly statistics, a parent had complained about clutter in the nursery, a teacher had taken all of the supplies for a project to be done by all classes, the weather was bad and attendance would be down.

Just then, four-year-old Beth blew into the foyer, pushed by the cold winter wind through the door opened by her father. She greeted Diane, sat down on a nearby bench, and pulled off her snowy boots. Then she jumped high into the air, and exclaimed as she scurried off toward her Sunday school classroom, "Oh, I just *love* it here!" Little Beth's enthusiastic affirmation of the importance of the church in her life was a lovely gift to Diane on that difficult morning. Beth's sense of belonging, begun at baptism and continued through the preschool years, had been nourished by the love of God through the ministries of that church. Suddenly, Diane's understanding of ministry revived and her flagging spirit renewed. Beth had given her a glimpse of God's love and presence.

At the very heart of our understanding of God is love. As Christians, we believe that all that is necessary is to love God (with our entire beings, all our minds and hearts and souls) and our neighbor.[3] Neighbor, as Christ defines it, is not only the person who lives next door, but any member of the human family, particularly those "in need." Further, we believe that all persons are "in need" in that everyone needs relationships to thrive. Loving one's neighbor means loving every person we touch through our lives and our work. Some we know and touch directly. Others we will never meet face-to-face.

To love God and neighbor is the heart of our faith and our theology.

The word *loving* does not necessarily mean the same for each person, obviously. Loving your family members and loving the stranger are different. But loving God and loving neighbor have particular meaning in regard to children. Loving children, caring for them, advocating for them, and taking action on their behalf are ways of loving God.

Five-year-old Sara's life began in very difficult circumstances. She was orphaned at birth and addicted to cocaine. Adopted by a loving parent, she was responding to the love she received in her new family, but she still seemed to walk to the beat of a different drummer. She often drifted away from conversations and sometimes distracted others with seemingly unrelated comments. One Sunday Charles was leading a Sunday school class for a small group of mixed-aged children that included Sara. They were learning the story of Jesus raising his friend, Lazarus, from death. Charles asked the group how they thought Lazarus must have felt when he saw Jesus. Sara quickly responded, "God must love me very much!" Then she laughed and did a little dance of joy, delighting all in the room. "Yes, Sara, God does love you very much and so do we," Charles said to her, feeling very deeply the truth in that statement. Teaching Sara, including her, guiding her, and affirming her were all ways of loving her and of loving God. To love God and neighbor is the heart of our faith and our theology.

Imago Dei

Those deep thinkers in the church over the ages have developed some other ways one can think about God in relation to children.[4] One is the understanding that humans are created in the image of God, often called *imago Dei*. Coming from Genesis 1:27, this idea does not mean that our human bodies are like God's. Rather, we humans image God in our moral and spiritual selves. Unlike other animals created by God, we have abilities that allow us to make moral choices and transcend our selves. Diane and Laura Dean understand that God creates everyone in God's image—including persons who are not adults: children. *Imago Dei*, created in God's image, gives great value, irreplaceable value, to each and every child. None are excluded.

Jesus extended the concept of *imago Dei* even further as he reached out to children in ways that were highly unusual for his time and culture. He told the disciples that welcoming "one such child"[5] was the same as welcoming the Christ and that welcoming Christ was the same as welcoming the One who sent him. Jesus was not suggesting that we be nice to children and greet them warmly every Sunday. He was not asking that we think good thoughts about children. Jesus had something far more important in mind. He told his disciples quite plainly that when they looked into the face of a child, they should see the face of Christ. That challenge comes to us modern-day disciples just as surely as it confronted the original Twelve. Just as Lazarus looked into the face of Christ when Jesus gave him new life so Charles and the other children in the story above looked at Sara and learned something about God.

Incarnation

Knowing that all children are created in God's image, it is possible to see and know God by seeing and knowing children. In the Old Testament, humans are continually promising God to be loving people and they continually mess it up. God keeps renewing God's promise of love for the people, and they repent and try again.

With the coming of Christ, a new covenant is made. God actually assumes human form in the person of Jesus, a baby born in Bethlehem.

The child is also called Emmanuel—God-with-us. This is the incarnation of God: God taking human form, strangely enough as a baby. God came to us a vulnerable and helpless child. Further, God came to us as a child from a despised neighborhood,[6] to an unwed teenaged mother far from home. The incarnation of God in the baby in the manger is another realization of God's love for children. How much stronger could God have been in this statement of love for the little ones, especially the poor and rejected of society?

Call to Justice

In the book of Micah, the prophet calls us to justice when he proclaims, "He has told you, O mortal, what is good; and what does the Lord require of you but to do justice, to love kindness and to walk humbly with your God?"[7] Micah and other prophets of the time of the Old Testament call us to justice through the Scriptures. Justice is an equal distribution of resources and opportunities. It is fairness and equity. It is obligation, our basic understandings of our responsibilities to others, and the nature of our love for all persons. It is choice, a personal prioritizing of the way we use our lives for the betterment of the world and other people. Justice has always demanded repentance and change. This is still true. Justice, in our time, requires systemic change. In addition to our understandings of *imago Dei* and incarnation, when we, the people of God, think about the nature of God we must also take into account our underlying call to justice.

Discussion of these issues is more extensive in the following chapters, but at the outset all of us in the church must be clear: the existence of poverty, inadequate health care, and other critical issues related to child well-being poses an underlying question of justice. How can we love God if we are not caring for the children? Because a child is a child, made in God's image and a vessel of God's spirit, adults must be advocates for them. Adults and congregations must take action on their behalf. Can anyone say they love God and yet not advocate for children? No, not if they believe in the God described in this chapter.

Such a change means moving from an understanding of justice as earned by social status and "deserved" to an understanding of justice like

God's grace: unearned and inclusive. Injustice marks the lives of many children! Nearly half of the world's children lives in poverty. Almost one-quarter of the world's children does not have basic immunizations against childhood diseases.[8] Many children both in the United States and around the world are left alone at home (or worse yet, in a car or on the street) because their parents must choose between going to work and caring for them. In a recent trip to India, Dr. Linda J. Vogel[9] described in email correspondence a six-year-old child, clad only in underpants, who spent her days with no supervision in miserable living conditions caring for her two-year-old and months-old siblings. Her mother had to work so they wouldn't starve. This is real, and it is unjust.

United Methodism and Children

John Wesley showed particular concern for the children of his eighteenth-century English society. He wanted to be sure that they learned the basic skills of reading, writing and arithmetic and that they came to know God and Jesus Christ. Clearly, Wesley cared about both the physical and spiritual well-being of children. He established free health clinics and schools for them and sought to address the economic and social problems of their parents. Among other things, he created work opportunities for poor women (mothers), such as sewing cooperatives, and set up a lending agency at a time when many men and women went to prison because of their unpaid debts.[10]

Wesley required Methodist preachers to spend time with children, mandating that preachers were to establish bands (a group of ten) of children and meet with them twice a week. When some of these early preachers indicated that they felt inadequate for such a task, Wesley responded, "Gift or no gift, you are to do it, else you are not called to be a Methodist preacher."[11]

The United Methodist Church has a long history of care, concern, and action for children, particularly those who live in poverty. Examples include the development of church school curriculum for all ages and teaching tools to support the work of Christian education teachers, the establishment of schools across the world and community agencies throughout the United States in high-need neighborhoods,

the organization of child advocacy networks by several annual conferences and at least two of the denomination's general (national) boards.
In addition, since 1988 the Campaign for Children,[12] has called attention to the needs of children, created opportunities for "hands-on" mission in local settings and, more recently, organized a focus on advocacy
with a special emphasis on public school education in the United States.

While several denominations of the Christian church in America
and the National Council of Churches have made statements concern-
ing the rights of children,[13] the Bishops' Initiative on Children and
Poverty (1996–2004) was a significant effort in The United Methodist
Church to increase mission and evangelism with and on behalf of children and the impoverished. Briefly, the emphasis by our bishops has
resulted in a denomination-wide "discussion" of children and poverty
and has had a profound impact on United Methodist people, congregations, and institutions.[14] New ministries have been formed, new
resources generated, and new studies written to help The United
Methodist Church understand and respond to children's issues and to
be in ministry with them, acting and serving as disciples of Jesus Christ
together. In the closing year of the Initiative, the Council of Bishops
published "Our Shared Dream: The Beloved Community," a theological document that envisions and moves toward a future in which we
realize the reign of Christ.

The Council of Bishops has focused on "making disciples of Jesus
Christ for the transformation of the world."[15] The bishops are leading
United Methodists throughout the denomination in learning about and
acting on what Jesus teaches about being a church in the world, making
a difference, transforming the world to look more and more like the
reign of God.[16] Earlier, in November 2005, the Council of Bishops
adopted seven vision pathways through which they will lead the
church:

- Developing new congregations.
- Transforming existing congregations.
- Teaching the Wesleyan model of forming disciples of Jesus
  Christ.
- Strengthening clergy and lay leadership.

- Reaching and transforming the lives of the new genera-
  tions of children.
- Eliminating poverty in community with the poor.
- Expanding racial/ethnic ministries.[19]

The Bishops are using these vision pathways as they give witness and leadership to their episcopal areas across the denomination. In addition, they referred these seven pathways to the Connectional Table and the general agencies of the denomination to guide their visioning, strategic planning, and funding work.

Closing Thoughts

Rev. Dr. Eileen Lindner, the Deputy General Secretary of Research and Project Planning from the National Council of Churches, told a story about one of her children who, when offered a drink of water from Eileen's own cup, asked, "If I drink of your cup will I catch your dreams?"[18] Her child's mistake in words was prophetic. How do we help children catch the dreams of the reign of God?

Powerful images—the beloved community, the peaceable kingdom, the *kindom*[19] of God, the world in harmony with itself—tell us about the reign of Christ. Each of these images points to the same dream and reality: justice and inclusion for all—the poor, the vulnerable, and the children. This is what God must think about children. They are equal and deserving of nothing less than all we have. Advocacy for children is an important road on the journey to this *kindom*.

This is not a theology book, but theology infuses this chapter and every chapter. Bear in mind, theology belongs to each one of us. Our efforts to understand the nature of God and the relationship we have with God and neighbor are an integral part of each Christian's everyday life.

Theology demands that we not only think about God but that we also act in response to God's action in our lives. God came to us in human form—as a child—to exemplify God's love for children. God through Christ is in every child. We see Christ in their faces and their actions. God asks only that we love God and one another. Serving children is serving God. Taking action on their behalf is action for God. Advocating for children is advocacy for God and hope for the realization of the *kindom* of God. This theology of justice and inclusion is the loom upon which we begin to weave the ministry of child advocacy.

Questions for Reflection

1. What stories can you tell about a child or a group of children understanding and discussing God's love for them? Can you think of an example of a child showing you God's love?
2. What images of God are helpful to you, or have great meaning to you? List as many as you can.
3. When have you felt great love and protection for children? What were the circumstances? How did you feel?
4. What are some examples of ways in which you recognize and experience children (and their parents) as your neighbors?
5. In what ways has your understanding of discipleship expanded to include "taking action for children?" What are some new things that you will do as a result of this change?
6. In what ways do you agree with this book's definitions of *imago Dei* and incarnation? What other thoughts do you have about these two concepts?
7. What would you add to this stated theology of child advocacy?

Action Steps

1. Read *Phase III: Public School Education*, the 2002 publication from the Campaign for Children of the United Methodist Women. Share it in a book group or write an article for your church's newsletter. If you are a member of a circle, share it with your program chairperson.
2. Download (www.umc.org, click on Council of Bishops) and read *"Our Shared Dream: The Beloved Community."*

Find out who in your annual conference is working on organizing efforts related to children and the poor. Invite them to share information and resources with your church.

3. Write down your own ideas about the nature of God. What do you believe about God? What does it mean to you to love God through your actions for children?

4. Think about starting a discussion or reading group at your church or in your neighborhood to talk about God and children. Begin with some of the questions for discussion, above.

Chapter 1 Notes

1. The theology in this chapter is informed by many sources, including David H. Jensen's *Graced Vulnerability*. See bibliography.
2. John Wesley's writings suggest the use of the quadrilateral—Scripture, tradition, reason, and experience—as a means of working out our theology and faith.
3. Matthew 22:37–39.
4. This understanding of the historical theology of our Christian church comes in part from learning at a Child Advocacy Institute of the Children's Defense Fund. The institute continues to be held annually in the summer. For more information see their website, www.childrensdefense.org.
5. Mark 9:33–37, Matthew 18:1–5, Luke 9:46–48
6. "Can anything good come from Nazareth?" John 1:46
7. Micah 6:8
8. Statistics from UNICEF, www.unicef.org.
9. Linda J. Vogel, email dated May 4, 2007, from Bangalore, India.
10. Drawn from an excerpt titled "Methodism, Children and the Poor," in *Children and Poverty: An Episcopal Initiative*, published by the Council of Bishops of the United Methodist Church, 1996. Quoted in *Community with Children and the Poor: A Guide for Congregataional Study* prepared by the Task Force for the Bishops' Initiative on Children and Poverty, 2003, 11–12.
11. Richard P. Heitzenrater, *Wesley and the People Called Methodists* (Nashville: Abingdon Press, 1995), 232.
12. The Campaign for Children is a ministry of the United Methodist Women
13. See, for example, www.pcusa.org for the Presbyterian Church's "A Vision for Children and the Church," 1993, and the Episcopal Church's "A Children's Charter for the Church, 1997," supplemented in 2003 with "Receiving the Child" Study Guide. See also the National Council of Churches "Church and Children: Vision and Goals for the 21st Century," 12/04, www.ncc.org

14. There is more discussion of the Initiative and the Beloved Community in chapter 10.
15. Tim Tanton, "Report of the May 1–6, 2006 meeting of the Council of Bishops of the United Methodist Church," United Methodist News Service, May 9, 2005.
16. Ibid., statement attributed to Bishop Bruce Ough in same article.
17. Tim Tanton, "Report on the October 30–November 4, 2005 meeting of the Council of Bishops of the United Methodist Church," United Methodist News Service, November 8, 2005.
18. This story was taken from notes on a sermon given at the Institute for Child Advocacy of the Children's Defense Fund in 1997. It has since been published in Linder's book *Thus Far on the Way: Toward a Theology of Child Advocacy* (Louisville: Witherspoon Press, 2006).
19. *Kindom of God* is another way to talk about the Kingdom of God, a primary focus of Jesus' preaching and teaching. *Kindom* is a term that came out of the social justice movement of the 1960s, where the Kingdom of God was reimagined in a way that focused on the interrelationship of all people in a nonhierarchical way. It is very similar in meaning to the peaceable kingdom or what we understand to be the reign of Christ.

CHAPTER 2

Hearing the Word

⪡ Faith Imperatives for Child Advocacy ⪢

Story

Marian Wright Edelman stands out in modern American history as a child advocate, and her faith is the foundation of her advocacy beliefs. She is the founder of the Children's Defense Fund. Her work has made differences in the lives of America's children for the past several decades. Edelman, in her book entitled *Lanterns: A Memoir of Mentors*,[1] discusses the lives and teachings of persons who have served as her mentors. Among them are her parents, who taught and shared their faith with her. She talks about seeing the face of God in her parents' faces, and knowing God's love through them. She also learned from them that people of faith must stand for those who are in need, to take action on the behalf of others, as well as to lean on her faith to sustain her. Justice, particularly justice for children, is at the heart of her ministry. She says over and over again in her writings, and by her example, that faith drives her life on behalf of children.[2]

Edelman makes it clear that persons of faith have no choice but to speak and act against injustice. In this chapter, we take a brief look at faith imperatives for child advocacy, that is, those elements and touchstones of our faith that compel us to take action for children. These are essential pieces of the loom with which we weave our fabric of advocacy. These include wisdom from the Bible and the stories of persons in Scripture, as well as the stories of persons from both ancient and modern history. These Scriptures and stories teach us much about what it means to be a child advocate. The stories make it clear that there is something in every story for us, yet not one story will become our entire story. There is still room for the work of the Spirit in our lives as we continue on our advocacy journey of faithful discipleship.

The Bible Stories

Our Bible is full of stories and sayings that help us understand and improve our relationships to one another and our relationship with God. From the very beginning, we are seen as beloved children of God, who do both great things and awful things as we struggle and dance through life. As child advocates, we find wisdom and guidance in every book of the Bible.[3] From Cain and Abel in Genesis 4, to the place in Genesis 33 where Jacob pleads to go "at the pace of the children" because they are weary, to the Gospels and their many references to children, we are informed for our ministries as disciples who are advocates for children. We are encouraged and sustained by stories such as the midwives of Moses' rescue and the urgent voices of the prophets who proclaim justice for the children of God.

In looking at the many kinds of references for child advocacy in the Bible, we found five primary categories: mandates for advocacy, proscriptions against harming children, inclusion of children, justice for children, and care for children. Some Scriptures may be seen in the light of more than one of these categories. Some could actually appear in all five. As you think about them for your own ministries, feel free to recategorize them or include others that have value and meaning to you. Our examples in this book echo our experiences and, we hope, will form a basis for your own reflection as you study and pray the Scriptures.

Biblical Mandates for Advocacy:

- Isaiah 28:16–17a: "therefore thus says the Lord God, See I am laying in Zion a foundation stone, a tested stone, a precious cornerstone, a sure foundation: 'One who trusts will not panic.' And I will make justice the line, and righteousness the plummet";
- Jeremiah 31:15b: "Rachel is weeping for her children; she refuses to be comforted. . . ."
- Zechariah 7:9–10: "Thus says the Lord of Hosts: Render true judgments, show kindness and mercy to one another; do not oppress the widow, the orphan, the alien, or the poor; and do not devise evil in your hearts against one another."
- Matthew 10:42: "and whoever gives even a cup of cold water to one of these little ones in the name of a disciple—truly I tell you, none of these will lose their reward."

Proscriptions against Harming Children

- Deuteronomy 27:19a: "Cursed be anyone who deprives the alien, the orphan, and the widow of justice."
- Proverbs 14:31: "Those who oppress the poor insult their Maker, but those who are kind to the needy honor him."
- Matthew 18:6–7: "If any of you put a stumbling block before one of these little ones who believe in me, it would be better for you if a great millstone were fastened around your neck and you were drowned in the depth of the sea. Woe to the world because of stumbling blocks! Occasions for stumbling are bound to come, but woe to the one by whom the stumbling block comes!"
- Matthew 18:10a: "Take care that you do not despise one of these little ones. . . ."
- Matthew 18:14: "So it is not the will of your Father in heaven that one of these little ones should be lost."

Inclusion of Children

- Deuteronomy 31:12: "Assemble the people—men, women, and children, as well as the aliens residing in your towns—so that they may hear and learn to fear the Lord your God and to observe diligently all the words of this law."
- Matthew 19:14, Mark 10:14b, Luke 18:16: "but Jesus said, 'Let the (little) children come to me, and do not stop them, for it is to such as these that the kingdom of heaven belongs."
- Matthew 18:5, Mark 9:37a, Luke 9:48a: "Whoever welcomes one such child in my name welcomes me."
- Acts 2:39: "For the promise is for you, for your children, and for all who are far away, everyone whom the Lord our God calls to him."

Justice for Children

- Micah 6:8: "He has told you, O mortal, what is good; and what does the Lord require of you but to do justice, and to love kindness, and to walk humbly with your God?"
- Deuteronomy 16:20a: "Justice, and only justice, shall you pursue."
- Psalm 10:17–18: "O Lord, you will hear the desire of the meek: you will strengthen their heart, you will incline your ear to do justice for the orphan and the oppressed, so that those from earth may strike terror no more."
- Matthew 25:38–40: "And when was it that we saw you a stranger and welcomed you, or naked and gave you clothing? And when was it that we saw you sick or in prison and visited you?" And the king will answer them, "Truly I tell you, just as you did it to one of the least of these who are members of my family, you did it to me. "

Care for Children

- Genesis 33:13–14a: "Jacob said to him 'My lord knows that the children are frail and that the flocks and herds, which are nursing, are a care to me; and if they are overdriven for one day, all the flocks will die. Let my lord pass on ahead of his servant, and I will lead on slowly, according to the pace of the cattle that are before me and according to the pace of the children,'"

- Matthew 10:42: "Whoever gives even a cup of cold water to one of these little ones in the name of a disciple—truly I tell you, none of these will lose their reward."
- Luke 11:11–12: "Is there any among you who, if your child asks for a fish, will give a snake instead of a fish? Or if the child asks for an egg, will give a scorpion?"
- James 1:27: "Religion that is pure and undefiled before God, the Father, is this: to care for orphans and widows in their distress and to keep oneself unstained by the world."

Biblical Images for Advocates

In addition to the references to child advocacy listed above, other stories in the Bible provide us with more complete images of an advocate's work. The Bible characters possess personal attributes that we can claim today as we advocate for children. Some of these are generosity, creativity, daring, and strength to confront authority. Four of these wonderful stories are summarized below, with our understandings of their implications for child advocacy.

Courage and Strength

Their names were Shiphrah and Puah, and they were midwives to the Hebrew women, enslaved in Egypt. The new king of Egypt ordered them to kill any male children born to the Hebrew women, because he was afraid of their growing numbers and possible strength. The text says that the midwives "feared God," which is usually meant as loved God. Because they loved God, they did not do what the king told them to do. When the king questioned them, they lied to him, blaming the strength of the Hebrew women for the live births. The midwives were strong and courageous in the face of authority. They knew the right thing to do because of their understanding of and faith in God. They acted against the king out of their love for God. (Exodus 1:8–22)

Initiative and Assertiveness

In this story, the prophet Elijah stopped on his travels at the home of a widow, who had one son, and asked for food and drink. The widow had very little and wanted to feed herself and son first from the little she had, but Elijah insisted that she make him a meal first. Then he said that in God's power, she would have enough to eat until the rains came. For the next days, they had more than they needed. But then the son became very ill, and died, causing the widow to become angry at God and Elijah. Even Elijah was perplexed at the death, asking why God would allow this tragedy. Elijah took the child to his bed where he laid his own body upon the boy three times and prayed for God to restore the boy's life. The boy revived. (1 Kings 17:8–24)

Both Elijah and the widow were advocates for the child in this story. The widow tried to keep him safe by ensuring that he would have enough to eat and by asking Elijah for help when the boy died. Elijah used prayer both to extend the food supply and to revive the boy from death. Further, he used his physical body to save him (an early version of CPR?). Finally, both the widow and Elijah, the prophet, were dismayed by the death of the boy—an injustice and a tragedy, and both took action against it.

Persistence and Speaking Truth to Power

A woman shouted at Jesus to have mercy on her because her daughter was being tormented by a demon. When he ignored her, she kept shouting. The disciples suggested that Jesus should send her away. She then knelt before him and asked for his help again. He responded by telling her it was not fair to take children's food and give it to dogs, and she said even dogs can eat the crumbs under the table. Jesus praised her faith, and the child was healed.

One of the first advocate's attributes we saw in that story is persistence. The woman would not give up, even though it must have been frightening for her. She was a Gentile, and Jesus was a Jew, whose mission had been to come to the Jews. Her persistence was brave persistence. It is surprising that she asked Jesus in the first place. She was looking for help for the child wherever she thought she could—even in a healing miracle from a stranger passing through the area where she lived. (Matthew 15:21–28)

Catalytic Connection

The story of Jesus feeding the multitudes of people near Tiberias is repeated in all four Gospels. In John's version, Andrew, one of the disciples, pointed out to Jesus that there was a boy who had five loaves and two fish. Andrew was the one who understood that a child's offering might have been exactly what was needed to feed the crowd, even though he didn't understand how. He asked, "But what are they among so many people?" Sometimes, even when we cannot express how changes can be made or what actions should be taken, we can still point out the gifts of the children in our midst and the children of the world. We can lift these gifts even if they appear, to us, to be insignificant. Further, we can connect the gifts or the needs of the children with the resources of adults and communities. (John 6:1–14)

Historical and Contemporary Images for Advocacy

The stories of many people in history and living today could be listed in this chapter, but we have narrowed it down to seven who show us diversity of age, race, and economic status as well as type of advocacy for children. Their stories are, like those of the biblical persons outlined above, brave, strong, persistent, and assertive. Their stories also bring us a sense of the great implications of one person's actions for children and the poor.

Harriet Tubman

Harriet Tubman put herself at great personal risk escaping from slavery and then helping others escape. Born a slave in 1819, Tubman escaped into Canada through the work of the Underground Railroad and became a leader in that movement, conducting more than 300 persons of all ages to freedom. After the Civil War, she worked in New York for women's rights, and in the last years of her life, turned her own home into a nursing home for the elderly and indigent. For additional information, see the New York History website.[4]

Anne Frank

Anne Frank was a Jewish teenager who lived in Amsterdam, and was forced into hiding during the Holocaust. During the two years of hiding, she wrote a diary that has become a widely read book.[5] Anne Frank died at Bergen-Belsen concentration camp in Germany in March, 1945. Her written words testify to her courage, understandings of justice and hope, and to our understanding of children who serve as advocates for children and others in need.

Trevor Ferrell

When Trevor Ferrell[6] was a third grader, he heard a news story about homeless persons who needed shelter on a very cold night. He thought it was referring to *a single* person, so Ferrell convinced his father to take him into Philadelphia to give the cold person a blanket. Instead he found thousands of homeless people. Trying to make a difference, he started a family effort, then a neighborhood one, and then a nonprofit organization dedicated to helping persons who are homeless with food, clothing, and more. In 1991, a movie titled *Christmas on Division Street* was made about Ferrell's work. Today he owns a thrift shop in Lancaster, Pennsylvania, and sometimes does public appearances on behalf of persons who are homeless and in need.

Ryan White

Born in 1971 with hemophilia, a disease of uncontrolled bleeding requiring transfusions, Ryan White[7] was diagnosed with AIDS in 1984. He was told he had no more than six months to live, and he wanted to live it with other children, going to school and participating in activities. His school officials, parents, and teachers were frightened by the disease, and they refused to allow him to attend school until the fall of 1986 when the courts ordered his acceptance. By this time, new drug treatments had become available, and the story was receiving national attention. A movie was made of his struggle to overcome the fear and prejudice people assumed against him. He publicly advocated for inclusion of people with HIV/AIDS, and the inclusion of persons with disabilities. In April 1990, Ryan White died of AIDS, and his parents and friends have continued his work through The Ryan White Foundation and a federal program that funds HIV/AIDS-affected persons.

Fred Rogers

Known as "Mr. Rogers" to millions, Fred Rogers was a child advocate. Rogers, an ordained minister, became a daily presence in the lives of children and adults through a television show, *Mr. Rogers' Neighborhood.* In a predictable welcome, each time the show aired, Mr. Rogers would enter singing a song about what it meant to be a neighbor, put on a comfortable sweater, and change into tennis shoes. He welcomed all into his neighborhood and throughout the show told children through his words and his way of being that they were loved and valued. His advocacy went far beyond the television show as he connected with the world in his gentle and loving way. He taught us much about how to be neighbors, to love children, and to help them be and become.

Part of the loom from which we weave child advocacy is the witness and learning from those who have gone before us.

Hillary Rodham Clinton

Hillary Rodham Clinton, who has been in public service for many years, has served faithfully as a child advocate. If you search on the Internet for "Hillary Clinton children," you will see hundreds of ways the work she has done over the past three decades has changed children's lives. According to the official biography for the U.S. Senate,[8] after the attacks of September 11, 2001, she worked to ensure assistance and compensation for the families of victims. She has since worked on legislation regarding safety of prescription drugs for children, health insurance for children, and safety at school, to name only a few. In addition, Hillary Clinton, who claims The United Methodist Church as her home church, has written a book on advocacy for children titled, *It Takes a Village and Other Lessons Children Teach Us,*[9] which urges us to care for all our children.

Margaret Mikol

We read the story of Margaret Mikol in a recent edition[10] of Time magazine, illustrating the reality of advocates in our lives today in very accessible ways. In 1978, she gave birth to a child, Julia, who had combined immunodeficiency, a disease that affects the immune system in such a way as to require a completely sterile home environment for the child. Systems then in place for caring for such children did not allow for the parents to care for them at home. Mikol battled the system until she was able to care for Julia in their home until she died at age eight. She then founded "Sick Kids need Involved People" (SKIP)[11], which has helped thousands of other families in similar situations. Mikol's work is not over. Her dreams for the future include a residential facility for respite for families with sick children.

The Loom

In every weaving, the loom is of great importance. It provides a base and sets the scale for the process of weaving. Part of the loom from which we weave child advocacy is the witness and learning from those who have gone before us, biblical persons and our contemporaries, and those who live among us today as our mentors, examples, and leaders. Their stories give us courage to take action on behalf of children.

Questions for Reflection

1. Look up several of the Bible passages we suggest as imperatives for action on behalf of children. Think about their meanings in today's world. For example, what might it mean to go at the pace of the children (from Genesis 33)? How would our world be different?

2. Think of other Bible stories that could be seen as examples of advocacy for children. Why do you think this is child advocacy? Is this a new insight for you, and, if so, how is it helpful to you? How is it your story?

3. Read Exodus 1:8–22, the story of the Hebrew midwives again. Think about the risk the midwives took by their failure to follow the orders of the king. When did you take a risk for a child? What did you need in order to take that risk? Courage? Strength?

4. Review our list of persons in "Historical Images for Advocacy." With whom do you identify with most closely and why? What do you learn for your ministry of advocacy from this person's life or actions?

5. We have described both biblical and contemporary/historical advocates as brave, persistent, assertive, and strong. In addition to these, what adjectives would you use to describe them? What adjectives would you use to describe your own advocacy efforts?

Action Steps

1. Identify another Bible character who takes action on behalf of children. Write an article for your church or organization's newsletter that describes this character's advocacy.

2. Identify another historical or contemporary person who takes action on behalf of children. Write an article for a newsletter or website describing the person and his/her contributions to child advocacy. Include encouraging words to help people see themselves in the story and take action.

3. Create a bulletin board or other visual display depicting the stories of biblical, historical, or contemporary models for child advocacy for your church or organization.

4. Begin a new column for your newsletter or website called "An Advocate to Notice" or "Work Worth Seeing," and

write the stories of persons in your church, conference, or organization whose advocacy efforts are changing the world for children.

Chapter 2 Notes

1. Marian Wright Edelman, *Lanterns: A Memoir of Mentors* (New York: Harper Collins Publishers, 1999).
2. See also Marian Wright Edelman, *The Measure of Our Success*, for an understanding of the influence of faith in her advocacy work.
3. For a Child Advocate's concordance to the Bible, see the Children Defense Fund's NRSV with a Child Advocate's Topical Concordance, Compiled by Shannon Daley-Harris, 1998.
4. See www.nyhistory.com/harriettubman/life.htm.
5. *The Diary of Anne Frank* was originally published in 1947. There are several versions, some listing Anne Frank as author while others list those who comment on the original diary. See www.annefrank.org.
6. From an article by Bob Gerth, December 4, 2003, at www.citypaper.net/articles/2003-12-04/cb2.shtml.
7. For additional information on Ryan White, see www.ryanwhite.com.
8. See this biography at http://clinton.senate.gov/about/biography/index.cfm.
9. Hilary Rodham Clinton, *It Takes a Village and Other Lessons Children Teach Us* (New York: Simon and Schuster, 1996).
10. Caroline Kennedy, "The Power of One: Rx: Home Care," *Time*, June 4, 2007, 57.
11. More information on SKIP is found at www.skipofny.org

CHAPTER 3

Understanding the World of Children

⫸ Assets and Needs ⫷

Story

Diane's office overlooks the playground of her church, where the children of the daycare center play several times a day. When the door opens and the children are released into the playground, they cheer and run happily to the swings and climbing equipment. From the window above, we can see and hear differences among the children. They are tall, short, fat, thin, blond, dark haired, with varied skin colors. We can hear different languages and accents, and laughter. Their behaviors vary. We know that some of the children take attention deficit disorder medications, some take asthma medications, and still others are in speech or physical development classes.

Several have allergies to various foods, especially nuts, and many have allergies to airborne pollutants. More than a third are living with one parent or living between parents. The others live with both parents, most of whom work outside the home, except for one who lives with his grandmother. Several have step-brothers and step-sisters, and most live a long distance from extended family, such as grandparents, aunts, and uncles.

These are typical children in today's American culture. Our faith tells us that all of them need affirmation, kindness, grace, and forgiveness, and an understanding of God's love through the people in their lives. Not yet five years old, they belong to a new generation, one that hasn't even been given a name by those who study such things. Still, we can make generalizations about them and their world that help us understand them as a group and as individual children, giving us basic facts that underpin the need for our advocacy.

Scripture

In Mathew 18:1–7, we read of Jesus teaching his disciples:

> At that time, the disciples came to Jesus and asked, "Who is the greatest in the kingdom of heaven?" He called a child, whom he put among them, and said, "Truly I tell you, unless you change and become like children, you will never enter the kingdom of heaven. Whoever becomes humble like this child is the greatest in the kingdom of heaven. Whoever welcomes one such child in my name welcomes me. If any of you put a stumbling block before one of these little ones who believe in me, it would be better for you if a great millstone were fastened around your neck and you were drowned in the depth of the sea. Woe to the world because of stumbling blocks! Occasions for stumbling are bound to come, but woe to the one by whom the stumbling block comes!"

As we, through this chapter, look to the realities of the world of children today, we see the role of advocates as those who remove the stumbling blocks in the paths of children.

Wellness Defined

Children are people whose ages range from birth to age 12 or so. With the decreasing age of puberty in many American children, one could say that childhood ends earlier than in previous generations, but for this book, we will consider childhood to extend to age 12. In the United States, according to data from the 2005 census,[1] there were more almost 48 million children under the age of 12 in the United States. In order for us to know how they are doing and what their needs are, we must look at the "whole" child, the physical, cognitive, emotional, and spiritual capabilities and needs of the child. We must understand children through a perspective that includes the mind, the body, and the spirit. Further, we must see them as part of various systems: family, community, and culture. These systems function, in part, to support and nurture the child through the provision of basic needs of the "whole" child, of the child's body, mind, and spirit.

We worked together a few years ago in an effort in the state of Illinois in a project through Voices for Illinois Children[2] to create a document called The Charter for Illinois Children. It outlined the basic needs of all children in the categories of education; family; economic security; health; safety; and arts, recreation, and culture to ensure that these needs were priorities among both private and public concerns. This was a holistic look at the needs of children in all aspects of their lives: body, mind, and spirit from which organizations and individuals were able to point to areas of advocacy. Children are not considered to be healthy or "well" unless needs are met in all areas. The work of child advocates requires that we see and understand the various systems that affect our children and point to those that need supplementation, mending, or perhaps even reconstruction.

In order for us to know how they are doing and what their needs are, we must look at the "whole" child.

In this chapter, we look at the large categories of family dynamics, community systems, and cultural perspectives as we describe the world of children of today. All of these categories play a role in preparing children for life, and each gives us, as advocates, understandings that help prepare us for our advocacy work. The last section of this chapter looks at crisis and how it disrupts and disturbs children's welfare.

Family Dynamics

Child-rearing practices

Parenting varies somewhat from generation to generation, and there are three possible generations who are parents of today's children. The baby boomer generation (those who are now in their 50s and 60s) are doting parents who sought "quality time" with their children, and the first generation of a large percentage of double-income families. Child care solutions were developed by this generation, whose children were often "latchkey" children, those who stayed alone at home after school until the parents returned from work. This is the generation that led feminist changes in America and initiated changes in gender roles in the home, particularly in child care. The baby boomers also tried to keep their children from experiencing failure. Such parents have been nicknamed "helicopter parents," a reference to the hovering they do around kids who seem unable to deal with problems and issues. In many cases this kind of parenting creates kids who cannot develop skills they need in later life. Currently, this generation of people is often either parenting their children's children or living in multigenerational households, or both.

Children of the baby boomer generation are of "Generation X," and are very protective (child kidnapping came into the national spotlight during their childhoods) and very concerned about how society influences their children. Dads and moms are both involved greatly in the day-to-day parenting of the children. Although both parents still need to work, there is creativity in working arrangements, including working from home, assisted by home computing and the Internet.

The Millennial generation is becoming parents, and their relationships with their own parents, as well as the ever increasing housing costs for young families in the United States today are creating multi-generational households. We predict that these parents will allow their children more creative and free time in response to their very structured childhoods. They are the first generation to have always lived in the computer age, and are eager for technological change and improvements.

Strengths (Assets) and Concerns

Given the varied nature of today's three generations of parents, there are still common strengths of families and common issues with which they struggle as they raise children in the United States. One in five children lives in a family with income below the federal poverty level. We have seen some improvement of the actual numbers of children in poverty over the past few years, but at this writing, there is an increase in poverty due to national economic issues.[3] We see impacts on lives by poverty's association with low birth weight children, limited educational opportunities, lack of access to health care, and more. Poverty is an indicator of many negative outcomes later in life.

Today's families in America have many strengths and tools to assist them. Information is readily available for decision-making and learning. Advances in technology mean that communication with family members becomes easier every day. Even extended family members are likely to be more involved than they were even a few years ago through communication by email and cell phones. Information for parenting, family life, child care, and more is instantly available via the Internet. Concerns are present with these technological advances, with great economic differences in the ability to have access and to use it. Families that do have the economic means to have computers in their homes, as well as those with televisions, are allowing children to spend hours per day in front of the TV or the computer. More than half of children now have TVs in their bedrooms, and the numbers with computers are not far behind. Lack of physical activity is clearly one of the reasons for the alarming increases in childhood obesity.

According to the U.S. Census Bureau,[4] the number of grandparents who head households in which their grandchildren live is up 19% from 1990, a rapid increase. More of these are grandmother-headed families, and about two-thirds of them also include one or more of the children's parents. Intergenerational families are often a strength for the children, with more adults involved in their lives. Yet, there are concerns raised by grandparent-headed families, particularly in those who are headed by a grandmother only, with neither grandfather nor parents of the children present. Data tell us that these families are likely to be poor (about two-thirds of them), and less educated.

In most working families in America, both parents work outside the home. As we know from the children in our own church child care ministries, children are apt to be away from parents for 10–12 hours a day, in child care or in a child care/school combination. Two-income households can be seen as strength for today's families, but can also be a concern in terms of time for the family to be together.

Rituals

A reality of family dynamics that can greatly enhance the lives of children is the likelihood in families of what we call rituals in their life together. Rituals are repeated behaviors that can create a sense of belonging, togetherness, and consistency. An example is the way a family celebrates birthdays—the same kind of pattern of celebration is often repeated year after year, and is anticipated and remembered. Another is bedtime. Children may go through a set of actions each and every night that serves to remind them that they are part of a family who cares for them, and they are comforted by the repeated words and actions, and the knowledge that they are safe within this family. A final example of rituals of families might also be in their use of faith rituals in the home. Prayers at meals and bedtimes, special remembrances of seasons of the year, such as Advent candle lighting in the home, and remembrances of death and life anniversaries in prayer and liturgy all point to security and belonging for children. These and other rituals strengthen families.

Concerns

Within every family of every type, there are a variety of concerns that affect the wellness of its children. Some of these are dealt with in more detail as "issues" in chapter 6, but are mentioned briefly here as a reality of family dynamics. The list is incomplete, as entire books could be written about the many concerns of importance to families today.

- Consumerism: Almost all families struggle with consumer decisions in a society now marketing to even very young children. All children in our culture are targeted by advertising almost every minute of every day. The newspaper that arrived as we wrote this morning was filled with ads aimed at children. For example, there is a large ad for a cell phone, with pictures of a 12-year-old on the front, and the words used to sell these phones include *fave, fun, check it out, hey,* and *hot.* Among the choices of wallpapers for the phone are cartoon designs. In a recent issue of *USA Today,*[5] an article pointed out how the film *Happy Feet* advocates for environmental change. At the same time, products, such as books, are using the characters of the movie to advocate for issues of inclusion in families. As parents, educators, and people of faith, but most of all as child advocates, we must be aware of the use of these kinds of advertising and promotion and help our children interpret them.

- Safety: In our ministries, we are seeing an overprotective group of parents and guardians who are reacting to child kidnappings and other child violence in somewhat unhealthy ways. We are calling this "The Safe Child Syndrome." Safety is a growing concern for families of all types, with abuse and neglect rates continuing at high levels, increasing violence against women, and fear of sexual and physical abuse of children. The Internet is proving to be a wonderful tool with a price. We recently received an email warning about Internet predators that recited a conversation between a young girl and a man posing as another girl. With very little conversation, the pretender was able to get the girl to give him enough information to determine where she attended school, her name, birthdate, and her address. Keeping children safe becomes "The Safe Child Syndrome" when no adults are trusted beyond a tight family circle, when children have little interaction with others, and when every part of their world is tightly controlled to keep them safe. We have families in our faith communities who will not trust our church nurseries and Sunday schools, preferring instead to keep the children close and safe with them at all times. We checked "safety" on the Internet just to see how much information was out there for families and were overwhelmed by the number of websites dedicated to child safety. Safety education and ensuring safe spaces is child advocacy.

- Media and Violence: Violence affects our children everywhere they go, at home, in the street, and in school. Violent video games are very popular in our American culture. At the holidays, persons were injured while stampeding to purchase the latest video game system, and new games bring new violence to children and youth. In a review of games in the *Minneapolis Star and Tribune*,[6] "maturity issues" raised by the games ranged from shooting to poisoning to mass destruction to obscenities. Sexual violence is seen nightly on the major television networks, and acted out among children in our schools. In the home, children are spending hours a day in front of the television and/or the computer. Families must learn to discriminate in the viewing and playing chosen for their homes.

Community Systems

There are many places in our communities that support and nurture children and their families. Among them are socioeconomic opportunities, support networks, schools, and other education-related institutions or groups, employment availability and diversity, and recreational opportunities. We believe that churches are able to support and nurture children in many of these places, and may become support networks and places for recreation as well as places of education and belonging.

It is difficult to describe all of the possible variations of these systems, so below we lay out a hypothetical set of community systems. These could assist each child advocate to begin to examine these community systems in their own settings and use them as lenses through which to see and understand the world of children.

The paragraphs below look at the hypothetical systems of a community called Anytown, a neighborhood of a large city in the northern part of the United States, in order to help us understand these community systems and their interdependence:

Socioeconomic

Anytown is a community of families who are new to the area, many of them immigrants from Mexico and Central America. It has always been a diverse community and originally had plenty of jobs in six large manufacturing plants and a large central shopping and entertainment district. Mass transportation has always been available via train through Anytown. About ten years ago, all but one of the manufacturing plants shut down, and a large percentage of the town's original residents left for jobs elsewhere, leaving a depressed real estate market. Many of the local businesses began to close, leaving vacant storefronts in the downtown area. Businesses with more affordable goods, like second-hand stores, began to move in.

Employment

Most of the current residents of Anytown work in other communities in service industries. Some still work in downtown stores and restaurants, in local schools, and protection services like police and fire. The remaining manufacturing plant recycles materials for furniture manufacturing and employs people of Anytown as well as a large percentage from other communities. About 12% of Anytown's workers are unemployed.

Support Networks

There are seven places of worship in Anytown, as diverse as the population. Each of these has its own ministries that support members and others, such as Alcoholics Anonymous, Parents Anonymous, and denomination-specific groups, but they also have formed a faith coalition that has recently begun a tutoring program at the elementary school. The community pages of the phone book show a variety of community-based programs such as Parents of Preschoolers, singles groups, and others.

Schools

The schools of Anytown are crowded and in need of updating. A recent tax levy failed to pass, which would have provided funds for hiring additional teachers and remodeling outdated areas of the elementary school, as well as adding a computer lab to the high school. The libraries of all of the schools do have computers for student and family use, but these are used at maximum capacity. Almost every weeknight, the schools are used for English as a Second Language (ESL) classes and other adult offerings.

Recreation

There is much green space in Anytown, and the park system is well used. Soccer and baseball are the primary children's sports, and there are school-related teams as well as more impromptu games. Often there are intergenerational games and many families gather on weekends for picnics and relaxation.

Summary

By understanding these systems of the community of Anytown, a child advocate can better understand the lives of individual as well as groups of children and then discern the needs of those children. For example, if the information above was all we knew about Anytown, we might determine that a good beginning place for our advocacy efforts is the elementary school, where we might begin by sponsoring a computer clinic, or by advocating for the passage of the next school levy, or by helping write grant applications for additional funding. The systems described above as well as systems of health care, government and administration, transportation, and commerce can all influence the needs of the children of a community. Time and effort in understanding them can greatly add to your effectiveness as a child advocate.

Cultural Perspectives

Cultural perspectives of families affect a child's well-being. Differing languages and customs of families migrating to the United States and assimilating create opportunities and challenges for our educational, health, and economic systems. On a statistical scale, ethnicity also affects a child's opportunities. According to the Federal Interagency Forum on Child and Family Statistics, poverty varies by race and Hispanic origin.[7] The poverty rates for White, non-Hispanic children in 2004 was 10%, 29% for Hispanic children, and 33% for Black children.

Children with immigrant parents are the fastest growing segment of the child population in this country, and their health and welfare are affected by their parents' access to systems of support, such as health care, employment, and education. If the current rate of growth among this segment of the population continues, one quarter of America's children will be of immigrant parents by 2010.[8] Children of immigrants live in families with lower incomes than children of natives, a situation created by language barriers, fear of authorities by unauthorized immigrants, and lower wages. On the other hand, immigrant families are often strong and supportive to one another and to others from their countries of origin, forming a support network that provides resources and maintains customs and language of their nativity.

Crises

A look at any newspaper on any day reminds us that natural disasters and similar crises have great impact on the lives and well-being of children. In light of recent events, such as hurricanes in the southern states and the post-traumatic stress created by the events of September 11, 2001, crisis is certainly a part of the state of the world as we and our children know it. In addition to these large-scale disasters, there are always smaller, more localized crises occurring: floods or tornadoes, fires, the closing of a major employer, and others.

A reality for our children is that natural disasters and crises of many kinds are some of the forces that "undo" all of the typical support systems for families, even those who are doing fairly well prior to the disaster. There is no place to turn for help, when home and employment and church and grocery store and friends all disappear at the same time. This "undoing" of the support systems adds to the lack of trust in the environment that children are feeling as a result of the initial impact of the disaster. For them, the world has changed dramatically. One of the most important tasks of adults, but particularly of child advocates during and after times of crisis, is to help rebuild a child's trust. This is done by providing a place of safety and assurance, of love and presence.

When you get right down to it, creating such safe spaces where children are free to receive God's love in many forms is what child advocacy is all about. Those forms include food when they are hungry, access to health care and education, safety, and opportunity. Children live in a tough and frightening world, and are unable to cope with that by themselves. Child advocates can change systems so that children will live a better future. This environment is the last component of the loom upon which we weave our fabric of advocacy for children.

Questions for Reflection

1. Looking at your own local community, what systems can you identify that are supporting and encouraging families with children? Create a list of at least five community systems and describe their benefits to children.
2. How do you define wellness for the children of your community?
3. What do you think are the most important strengths needed by a family in your community or church? List at least three.
4. Which are the cultural challenges facing families today?
5. The authors suggest that consumerism is a concern for families. Do you agree or disagree? Think about the implications of consumerism and the children for whom you are concerned.
6. Where is violence most evident in your community? If you were to try to make a difference, make the community less violent, how would you begin?

Action Steps

1. Think about the children of your church or your community, and write a list of what you know about them.

Include the "whole" child, attributes of body, mind, and spirit.

a) Create another list next to it of strengths and needs of the families of children you described.

b) Next to that list, on the same page, write what you think the community offers them in terms of the systems that support families with children. Include any insight you might have on cultural differences or needs of specific groups of families.

c) Save these lists for use later in the book as you develop your plans for child advocacy.

2. What sources for data can you find for understanding the children of your community? Create a file for a list of websites and agencies you can use as sources of information. You might organize these lists by topic or geographic area.

3. Review the generational theory information in a book such as *Making God Real for a New Generation*, by Craig Kennet Miller and MaryJane Pierce Norton.[9]

Chapter 3 Notes

1. Children Characteristics, U.S. Census Bureau, http://factfinder.census.gov.

2. Voices for Illinois Children is a nonprofit organization advocating for children in the State of Illinois. Its website is: www.voices4kids.org.

3. Austin Nichols, "Understanding Recent Changes in Child Poverty", The Urban Institute, www.urban.org/UploadedPDF/311356_A71.pdf, August 2006, accessed July 8, 2008.

4. U.S. Census Bureau, www.census.gov.

5. Michael Medved, "Preschoolers and Penguins: Propaganda Pawns" *USA Today*, November 29, 2006, 13A .

6. Randy A. Salas, Review of Video Games, *New York Times*, November 5, 2006.

7. American's Children in Brief, Federal Interagency forum on Child and Family Statistics, http://childstats.gov, 2004.

8. The Urban Institute, "Children of Immigrants: Facts and Figures," May 2006.

9. Craig Kennet Miller and Mary Jane Pierce Norton, *Making God Real for a New Generation* (Nashville: Discipleship Resources, 2003).

Practices, Issues, and Tools

CHAPTER 4

Welcoming Children

≋ Dimensions of Advocacy ≋

Story

Four ten- and eleven-year-old boys began "hanging around" the front steps of a small church in Chicago several years ago. A number of church members worried about their presence. Opinions ranged from "They might get hurt" to "Don't they have anything better to do?" Some persons wanted to tell the boys to stop coming to the church, but others insisted that the congregation should welcome them. A turning point came when a group of older men invited the boys to join their chess club. To the congregation's surprise, the boys started coming to the church on Friday evenings to play chess. After some months, other boys in the neighborhood asked to join the chess club.

Playing chess was an unexpected catalyst. Relationships grew between the two groups, and the men soon realized that these boys had other interests and needs. A couple of other church members started a drop-in computer literacy program. Girls joined the computer classes, and a few of them also learned to play chess. Some of the youth began attending worship services on Sunday and the outreach committee offered a homework assistance program after church every Sunday. Efforts to build relationships with their families increased, and a group of business professionals developed strategies to encourage the young people to stay in school, including a small scholarship fund to help them go to college.

Scripture

> People were bringing little children to him in order that he might touch them; and the disciples spoke sternly to them. But when Jesus saw this, he was indignant and said to them, "Let the little children come to me; do not stop them; for it is to such as these that the kingdom of God belongs. Truly I tell you, whoever does not receive the kingdom of God as a little child will never enter it." And he took them up in his arms, laid his hands on them, and blessed them. (Mark 10:13–16)

The disciples were probably very surprised by Jesus' reaction. They thought they were doing the right thing. After all, Jesus was busy, and he was probably tired. They had had a long day. Mark's account tells us, "And crowds again gathered around him; and, as was his custom, he again taught them." (Mark 10:1b) Sometimes people in the church today assume, just as the disciples did many years ago, that Jesus' message is for the adults. Jesus, however, had a different view. Jesus made it clear that children were an integral part of his ministry. Most important of all, Jesus took time for these children that day: "And he took them up in his arms, laid his hands on them, and blessed them." (Mark 10:16)

Types of Advocacy

We have already stated that advocacy is speaking, pleading, acting on behalf of another. Such a definition may lead us to think of advocacy as a single act, but, in most cases, advocacy is the *process* of taking action for an individual or a group of people. Advocacy for and with children—those who have neither voice nor vote—is always important. For Christian disciples, however, the mandate for child advocacy comes directly from Christ. Jesus—more than once—demonstrated his deep commitment to ministry with and advocacy for children.

> *Advocacy is the* process *of taking action for an individual or a group of people.*

Over a period of three years, Laura Dean has had the opportunity to observe a mid-size suburban church grow in its understanding of advocacy. Trinity-Grace has a membership of about 400 and includes children and adults across the age span. The congregation operates a full-time child care center for working parents, offers a variety of Christian education opportunities for all ages, gives generously to local, conference, and global missions, and facilitates opportunities for individual members to support or participate in a wide range of worthy organizations and missions.

The pastor, Steve, has served Trinity-Grace for about seven years. He has always affirmed the value of the church's various ministries, but he also recognized that some in the congregation often had difficulty making an explicit connection between their personal faith and the outreach ministries in which they were involved. Steve felt called to lead the congregation to a new place. His leadership and the church's journey give us some important insights into the multidimensional nature of advocacy. Trinity-Grace's experience demonstrates that advocacy usually falls into four categories:[1]

Type of Advocacy	Explanation	Example
1. Education	Learning about needs or issues, identifying resources, and raising awareness of others	Newsletter articles about the children in your community without health insurance
2. Service	Developing or working in programs that serve children and families, especially those who live in poverty	Vacation Bible school at a shelter for children of homeless parents or victims of domestic violence
3. Public policy	Promoting policies, legislation, and funding that support the well-being of children, youth, and families	Bill calling for legislators to increase child care services for low-income, working parents
4. Coalition[2] building	Working with others to address community problems or to create productive community relationships	State- or community-wide organization dedicated to improving public education

Education

Raising awareness of issues that affect the well-being of children and their families is an important way to advocate for children, but it is not an easy task. Steve points out that it is often difficult for people to grasp complex child and family issues that do not affect them directly. Such issues may feel distant or abstract and require a lot of interpretation. In other words, knowing that there are over two million reports of abuse or neglect every year in the United States rarely translates into a call to action to prevent child abuse in one's community.

Steve believes that hands-on experiences create the crucial link between an abstract issue (e.g., child abuse) and direct action to respond to that issue. For that reason, he introduced youth and adults to the Appalachia Service Project (ASP)[3] several years ago and has also involved each confirmation class in serving food every fourth Sunday at a church dinner for homeless and hungry people. He also made several attempts to create a "place" in the church in which people could discuss complex social issues. His informal conversations with church members stimulated some interest, but his proposal to the Church Council to organize a social justice group received limited support.

Steve tried another approach. He organized a team of three lay persons—a teacher, a social worker, and a businessman with international experience—to lead a Lenten study using *Community with Children and the Poor: A Guide for Congregational Study.*[4] Sara, Lindsey, and Derek had long discussions with Steve and with each other as they planned the study sessions. They discovered that they did not always agree with one another, and they found some of the concepts and stances of the study guide to be challenging and even controversial. They were particularly stymied by the session on global economics. Derek agreed to lead the session even though he questioned some of the study guide's analysis of globalization and its relationship to poverty, locally and globally. During the session, he shared some examples of his own experience in poverty reduction and economic development initiatives in other countries.

Using Micah 6:8 as the text, Steve preached a series of sermons during Eastertide as a follow-up on the issues discussed during the Lenten study: "[God] has told you, O mortal, what is good; and what does the Lord require of you but to do justice, and to love kindness, and to walk humbly with your God?" In the last sermon of the series, Steve challenged the congregation to "walk humbly with God" by making a commitment to *act* on the important issues of justice and mercy in their congregation, community, and world. This time, 14 people stepped forward. Trinity-Grace was moving to a new place in its understanding of discipleship and advocacy.

Service

Developing programs or working in programs that serve children and families is a natural outgrowth of educational advocacy. Service advocacy sometimes happens quickly. A group of people in a local church identify a social justice issue (e.g., school failure, violence reduction) and move quickly to initiate a new program or to create a partnership with a community agency already addressing that issue. In other situations, the development of service advocacy emerges over a longer period of time. Such was the case at Trinity-Grace.

For several months, the 14 individuals talked and prayed with one another and Steve in a number of conversations in a variety of settings. Leaders moved in place, and gradually, Micah Ministries took shape. The group adopted a five-step format to guide its work:

- Propose—suggest and agree upon issues for the group's study and action
- Learn—gather information and discuss a variety of perspectives
- Discern—consider the relationship between the issues and their discipleship
- Respond—develop and implement action strategies
- Engage—encourage others in the congregation to join their efforts.

After considerable prayer and discussion, Micah Ministries identified hunger as the issue on which they would focus their efforts. The group researched statistics on hunger and initiated support for a local food pantry. The United Methodist Men's group recruited church members to participate in a gleaning project organized by the Society of St. Andrew,[5] an organization committed to ending hunger through gleaning fields and donating the food to agencies that serve people who live in poverty. A couple of other persons in the congregation began serving as volunteers at the local food pantry. Momentum for action on hunger issues grew at Trinity-Grace. As their understanding of hunger increased, members gained a new appreciation for the confirmation class's monthly trip to a church in a low-income neighborhood in Chicago to serve a meal to homeless and hungry people.

Public Policy

Public policy advocacy involves promoting policies, legislation, and funding that support the well-being of children, youth, and families. Many congregations rarely see public policy as an integral aspect of their ministries. In fact, a number of church members believe quite strongly that churches should never get involved in public policy issues. We will discuss this issue more fully in chapter 8, but, for now, Trinity-Grace's experience will be instructive.

On a number of occasions, Steve urged Micah Ministries to consider the root causes for hunger and suggested that the group explore the extent of hunger in the church's suburban community. Instead, they wanted to relieve the immediate suffering of people who are hungry. Some members of the group did not see a public policy connection to hunger. Instead, they focused on direct service. They did not explore the hard question, "Why are there hungry people in our relatively affluent community?" Nor did they consider the related question, "Why is hunger a critical issue for so many children, youth, and families, some of whom live in the wealthiest nation in the world?"

Participation in 40-Hour Famine[6] helped the youth of the congregation make the connection between personal issues and public policy decisions. Throughout the weekend, the youth studied, prayed, worked, and played, but they did not have the snacks and meals typically found at a youth retreat. Instead, they packed the food that they would have eaten into boxes and delivered the boxes to a local food pantry. They recognized that their hunger pangs, although intense and uncomfortable, were temporary, and they tried to imagine what it would be like to be hungry all the time. They cut out paper dolls to represent the 29,000 people who die every day across the world due to hunger-related issues.

As their forty hours drew to a close, several youth asked an important question: "What can we do to end hunger?" As suggested in the World Vision guide for a 40-Hour Famine, the youth decided to write letters to the president expressing their deep concern for people who do not have enough food. They asked him to urge Congress to increase funding for federal food programs. The youth brought their paper-doll banner to the next worship service, and they read some of their letters to the congregation before mailing them to the president. Impressed by the action of the youth, several adults suggested that the entire congregation write letters about hunger.

Two years later, Micah Ministries sponsored a letter-writing campaign as part of the nationwide Offering of Letters organized by Bread for the World[7] every year. A number of adult church members wrote letters to their Senators during the worship service. The witness of the youth who participated in the 40-hour Famine had generated a turning point for the congregation.

Coalition Building

Working with others to address community problems or social justice issues is the fourth dimension of advocacy. Building coalitions increases cooperation in a community (or among several churches), promotes productive community relationships, and engages a larger cadre of people in efforts to ameliorate the complex problems for children, youth, and families.

The people of Trinity-Grace are just beginning to think about how they might work in coalition with others. As an initial step, Richard and Sue met with the staff of the child care center to explore how hunger affects the families in the program. Plans call for developing a brochure to distribute to all parents about food resources in the community. Tom and Jeanne have suggested that their efforts could reach more hungry people if Micah Ministries collaborated with other groups in the community. They have met with the steering committee of a nearby ecumenical food pantry to explore ways they might work together.

Mary and Rochelle, also active in Micah Ministries, have joined Protestants for the Common Good,[8] a statewide organization that educates and mobilizes laity and clergy to advocate with local and state elected officials on social justice issues. A friend of Steve's has also suggested that Micah Ministries get in touch with RESULTS,[9] a national organization that trains volunteers to advocate with their public officials and the media to inspire members of Congress to be leaders in the effort to end hunger.

Trinity-Grace is also considering becoming more active in United Voices for Children (UVC),[10] a coalition of the four child-serving agencies in the Northern Illinois Conference. UVC encourages churches to support the agencies and to appoint a child advocate in every congregation. The child advocate keeps the local church informed about child well-being issues and organizes responses to those issues.

Dimensions of Advocacy

The Mark passage at the beginning of this chapter presents a powerful example of how a child advocate functions. Jesus stopped in the middle of his busy schedule and welcomed both the children and their parents. He admonished the disciples for turning them away, and he demonstrated the importance of children as he embraced and blessed them. Following the example of Christ, child advocates speak, and they also act. Advocates pray, and they reach out to others. Advocates plead for a cause, and they organize a response.

Focus

Advocacy may concentrate on an individual or a group. Individual advocacy is the process of intervening or acting to address the needs of a specific child, youth, or family. In other words, if you know a 10-year-old who has been expelled from school for disruptive behavior and you support his mother's efforts to obtain mental health or tutoring services for him, you are doing individual advocacy.

Clearly, faithful individuals and congregations carry out—and expand—their advocacy efforts in countless, creative ways.

In another situation, you engage in group advocacy when you meet with the principal, speak at a school board meeting, or raise your concern at a PTA meeting about obtaining a counselor or mental health specialist for all of the students who need those services. Another form of group advocacy is to work on a broad issue that has an impact on a larger segment of the community. For example, you might join a coalition that plans to protest the proposed merger of two community hospitals by consolidating the operations of the two institutions at one location and leaving one community without a hospital.

Ethel, an older adult member of Laura Dean's church, tells a compelling story about her involvement in advocacy on behalf of an individual. For several years Ethel volunteered at the Street Youth Ministry (SYM) that operates near the church. SYM provides meals and health care for homeless youth living on the streets. One winter night, SYM served the usual soup and sandwiches to a group of youth near a busy intersection in the community. One young man, Jaime, sat down on the curb to eat his simple meal. As he ate his sandwich, a police car pulled up beside him and two officers jumped out of the car and grabbed him. SYM staff and volunteers watched in horror as the police handcuffed Jaime and pushed him roughly as he protested and struggled to free himself. The SYM members learned later that the police suspected him of dealing drugs, and the officers arrested him even though they did not find drugs on him when they searched him. He was jailed that night, and he did not receive medical attention for his injuries until the next morning.

When Jaime's pre-trial hearing came up, twelve volunteers from the Street Youth Ministry—including Ethel—attended. Three of them spoke on Jaime's behalf, and several SYM staff and volunteers came to every hearing until the judge dismissed the charges. With the conclusion of the case, Jaime's court-appointed lawyer said that he had underestimated two things. First, he was surprised by the level of commitment the advocates exhibited, and he also believed that their ministry of presence for Jaime had an impact on the outcome of the case. It seems that the judge was also impressed with the amount of advocacy they did for this young man. Jaime now has a job and a temporary place to live, but he still spends time with his friends in the SYM.

Commitment

In Jaime's situation, several people joined forces to advocate on his behalf, but there are other times when you must step out on your own to advocate for children. You may be the only person in your family or your church to recognize a particular child or family issue in your neighborhood. You may expect (or want!) someone else to speak up about that issue. You may feel inadequate to the task or unclear about what course of action to take. You believe the cause is too big for you, but if you do not tackle it, how can you know that someone else will? Through prayer and meditation, you will find a way to respond and act.

Another time, you may work with others who care about an issue close to your heart. The impetus might come from a mission study in your church or from a discussion at the church council. Through these conversations, you might identify several other persons who share your interest and want to work with you. In this situation, you have several options: organize a task force in your church, join the work of a coalition that shares your passion, or work with others to organize such a coalition! Many well-known coalitions across the country started because an individual or a small group of persons felt called to step out in faith to advocate on behalf of a particular cause. For example, fifteen women printed 1,000 Mother's Day cards to send to members of Congress in 1967. By the end of May that year, they had sold 200,000 cards, and Another Mother for Peace was born.[11]

The loom is no longer empty. Advocates have placed the first warp threads on the loom, and now we can begin weaving. The men in the chess club brought the ability to welcome and build relationships to the loom, and SYM added the power of presence. Trinity-Grace contributed hands-on learning, Bible study, clergy and lay leadership, and the witness of youth. Clearly, faithful individuals and congregations carry out—and expand—their advocacy efforts in countless, creative ways.

As you read the next chapters, keep in mind that advocacy takes many forms—praying and including, assessing and promoting, caring and defending, befriending and protecting, challenging and witnessing. Advocacy is all those ordinary and extraordinary actions that we weave together to create a better world for children and youth.

Questions for Reflection

1. Make your own list of words that describe advocacy. What are the surprises on your list? Mark the words with which you have the most resonance, or about which you feel strongly or feel capable of doing. Include these words in your prayers and meditations over the next three to six months. Expect new insights as you talk with and listen to God with these words.

2. Talk with others in your congregation about what it means to welcome children when adults are talking about important theological or public policy matters. Discuss some new ways in which to welcome children—those you know and those from the wider community—into your congregation's life and ministry.

3. Identify some examples of service advocacy in your local church or community. What specific (individual) dilemma did this program focus on initially? Has the program expanded over time to "take on" other problems of the families or community? If not, what are some ways that this program could be expanded to address the broader, root causes of the identified problem(s)?

4. What kind of skills does your church or community group need in order to get involved in a community-wide (or larger) coalition? How does being a "connectional" church help us to organize or join a coalition-building effort?

Action Steps

1. Conduct several interviews in the community surrounding your church to find out some of the ways community people are addressing critical child and family issues. Ask the persons that you interview to identify ways in which members of your congregation might become involved in their endeavors.

2. Find out what legislation has been proposed related to the community issue(s) that emerged through your conversations with community residents and leaders. Consider whether the legislation, if enacted, will be supportive of children and their parents or will it make their situations more difficult. Share that information with your congregation.

3. Get to know the policy makers who represent your local ward, state legislative and congressional districts. Write, call, and visit them to let them know your passion for children and your concern about proposed legislation or policies.

4. Identify ways to work in concert with parents as they search for the resources their children need in order to grow up strong and healthy, have good early childhood experiences, succeed in school, and find useful summer activities.

Chapter 4 Notes

1. A similar description of the four types of advocacy was published in Laura Dean Ford Friedrich, *Putting Children and Their Families First: A Planning Handbook for Congregations* (New York: General Board of Global Ministries, 1997).

2. A coalition is a combination or an alliance, especially a temporary one among persons, groups, or organizations.

3. Appalachia Service Project is a Christian ministry that makes homes warmer, safer, and drier for families in need in Central Appalacia while offering transformational experiences for families, volunteers, and staff alike. Contact ASP, Inc., at 4523 Bristol Highway, Johnson City, TN 37601-2937, 423-854-8800, www.ASPhome.org.

4. *Community with Children and the Poor: A Guide for Congregational Study* was developed by the Task Force for the Bishops' Initiative on Children and Poverty of the Council of Bishops of The United Methodist Church in 2003 and published by Cokesbury. Contact Cokesbury at 800-672-1789 or at www.cokesbury.com to obtain the study guide.

5. The Society of St. Andrew is a Christian ministry dedicated to gleaning America's fields and feeding America's hungry. Best known for its potato project, the Society also includes a nationwide gleaning network and sponsors the

Harvest of Hope Project, a weekend gleaning and study experience. Contact the Society of St. Andrew at its national office at 3383 Sweet Hollow Road, Big Island, VA 24526, 434-299-5956, 800-333-4597, www. endhunger.org.

6. The 30-hour or 40-hour Famine, developed by World Vision, helps churches, youth groups, and individuals learn about and address the issue of hunger. World Vision is a Christian humanitarian organization dedicated to working with children, families, and their communities worldwide to reach their full potential by tackling the causes of poverty and injustice. For more information, visit www.worldvision.org or www.30hourfamine.org.

7. Contact Bread for the World for information about the Offering of Letters at 50 F Street, NW, Suite 500, Washington, DC 20001, 202-639-9400, www.Bread.org

8. See Chapter 8 for more information about Protestants for the Common Good or visit www.thecommongood.org.

9. RESULTS is an international citizens' lobby whose purpose is to create the political will to end hunger, at home and abroad. RESULTS advocates for increased funding and replication of cost-effective programs that positively affect the lives of the poor. Contact RESULTS at 440 First Street, NW, Suite 450, Washington, DC 20001, 202-783-7100, www.results.action.org.

10. Contact United Voices for Children at Gary Memorial United Methodist Church, 224 N. Main Street, Wheaton, IL 60187, 630-668-3100, www.um voices4kids.org.

11. Learn about Another Mother for Peace at www.anothermother.org/history.html.

CHAPTER 5

Going Places We Never Expected to Go

⚔ Venues for Advocacy ⚔

Story

Often throughout life, we find ourselves going to places we didn't expect to go. Kelly grew up in a very affluent area of Chicago, and all of her education and the opportunities of life pointed to a successful career in her father's law firm. After graduation from college, she and her friends took vacation time in Europe before law school began in the fall. In London, Kelly separated from the group to return to the hotel, tired from the long day of sightseeing. As she traveled back, she found herself in an unfamiliar neighborhood and stopped to get her bearings. Just beyond where she stopped, a child was crying in a doorway. She walked over, and soon determined that the little girl was lost. Going door to door to find someone who knew the girl proved fruitless, but

Kelly decided not to leave the child alone again. They were finally directed to the nearest police station. After several hours, the child and mother were tearfully reunited, and Kelly was escorted to her hotel by the girl's grateful relatives. Kelly points to this short afternoon of advocacy for a child as a turning point in her career. She has given most of her working life as a full-time legal advocate for children.

Scripture

In the Gospels of Matthew, Mark, and Luke, we find a story of Jesus being called out of his teaching to heal a child. Jairus, a leader of the synagogue, interrupted Jesus to ask him to go quickly to his house, as his daughter was very ill (or has just died, in Matthew). Jesus went to the house and restored her to life. This is one of several stories in the Bible where people go to unexpected places to advocate for children. Think of the Hebrew midwives in the story of Moses and the mother who said "even dogs eat the crumbs under the table." Jairus certainly never thought he would kneel in the street at Jesus' feet. Jesus didn't plan his day thinking he'd be going to Jairus's house; nor did the disciples think this. It was not on their "to do" list. But the faith they taught and lived is not only about loving oneself and God, but about loving neighbor, especially those who are in need. Indeed, loving God is achieved through loving others.

In most organizations today, we have plans and vision statements that enable us to "see" where we are going, and often these plans include advocacy for children in some form. But just as Kelly's life was changed by her advocacy for the lost child, so are our plans changed by advocacy opportunities we didn't (or couldn't) see when we wrote the plans. In this chapter, we discuss venues for advocacy through two primary lenses, the church and the world beyond the church. We may write advocacy initiatives into our strategic plans, but know we must still be open to responding to the child who takes us by the hand and urges us to act.

Advocacy in the Church

Some people say advocacy in the church for children is very obvious. Since advocacy is taking action that makes a difference in the lives of children, churches can advocate for children by ensuring that the children of the church are well cared for, are safe in the church, and have access to that which they need for healthy life. The church can also advocate for children by offering ministries that help children and families build faith and express their discipleship. All of those tasks are actions for children; all will help the children they serve.

Another aspect of advocacy in our churches is seen through the way children are included in the community of faith. Churches know that Jesus said, "Let the children come to me," (Mark 10:14b) and respond to this verse by offering nursery care and Sunday school—maybe Wednesday afternoon programs, too. Many include children in worship services, many welcome children at the communion table. There is, however, much more to inclusion and welcoming than programming and allowing children to participate in adult worship. Welcoming children requires building a culture of inclusion.

At First UMC several years ago, there were few children. Those who were part of the church family were relegated to Sunday school classrooms while they were present. None had leadership roles. None served others in planned and organized ways. Clergy and lay leadership initiated intentional efforts that led to new understandings of inclusion of children in the life of the congregation. They became involved in leading worship and assisting with services by ushering, greeting, singing, or playing instruments. One child, Daniel, with the help of an adult usher, learned to direct people for communion services. Each time he learned that we were serving communion that day, his eyes lit up, and he stationed himself at the proper doors where he could do what he called "his" job of ushering. Daniel had learned that he was valuable in this capacity. Further, he "owned" this understanding of being included as a part of his faith journey. As he grew older, he expected this kind of inclusion, and, no doubt, offered it to others.

At about the same time, an adult usher was overheard in a service suggesting that a mother with a talking child take advantage of the nursery care offered during the service, rather than allow her child to ask questions *out loud* during a service. Persons sitting nearby were outraged at the usher's suggestion and told him so as they left the service that day. Comments ranged from "How else will he learn?" to "I've been more often interrupted by the shrill ringing of Joe's hearing aide than the questions of a child!"

The entire community at First UMC had learned to include children as they are, as valued and contributing worshiping members of the church. Over time, this kind of advocacy, making a difference in the lives of children by including them holistically in the life of the church, created a congregation that expected inclusion. Likewise, the inclusion of children in important ways created advocates in the congregation who would speak up for them and support them, creating a circle of love and making a difference in the lives of both children and adults. The church's understandings of leadership and of membership were redefined by their advocacy for children. The responses of children to this level of inclusion added to their knowledge of God through inclusion in the community of the church, strengthening their faith for life.

> *Advocacy includes being hospitable, allowing for and facilitating child leadership as well as participation.*

Part of the church's role in advocacy within the church itself is to work against ageism. Most people think ageism is discrimination against older people, making jokes that ridicule older people, or simply the lack of inclusion of older people in the church's ministries. Ageism often seen in churches, however, is discrimination against children and youth. Assumptions are made that children are all alike (noisy and squirmy), that youth are loud and disinterested, and church policies reflect this kind of ageism. Doing advocacy for children in the church means taking a stand against ageism directed against children or older people or anyone else. Jesus loves us all equally and invites us all to the table, whether we are five or ninety-five.

Children give the gift of life to the church, both literally through their beings and figuratively through our investment in them as future adults. In this time, especially, we must be attentive to our advocacy efforts. The largest generation of people now in childhood is called the Millennial Generation, and it is bigger than at any other time in the history of the United States.[1] At the time of the writing of this book, they are in a "youth boom"; the Millennial Generation comprises anyone aged eight to 25. The size of this generation affects consumer choices, music, and beliefs. Further, they have access to information we never dreamed of even a decade ago. Information gives children opportunities to make choices other than church, and many are doing so. One piece of really good news for the church is that this generation of children is made up primarily of "joiners," persons who want to join and belong to groups they believe are making a difference. According to *USA Today*,[2] children and youth today know what's going on in the world, and feel a need to make a difference in it. The terrorist attacks in New York and Washington on September 11, 2001 were very influential in forming this generation of young people in their attitudes toward service. They are service-minded as volunteers and work to help others in trouble. The events of 9/11 also contributed to this generation's knowledge of fear and uncertainty.

The next generation,[3] those born from 2001 until the present, will not be as large and will have its own big issues and challenges. We do know, based on our understanding of generational theory and our grasp of demographic trends, that children make up a large percentage of church people, and they bring issues unique to each generation. Advocacy includes being hospitable, allowing for and facilitating child leadership as well as participation. It requires paying attention to the changes created by the influence of these generations.

Realities of Various Environments

Differences exist among various sizes of churches and in the cultural locations of churches. The demographic characteristics of the neighborhood, physical location and proximity to other buildings and park areas, and resources available in the setting all contribute to the environment from which advocates may respond. Urban churches, for example, are often "landlocked." They may not be able to find space for parking, and many cannot expand their facilities or renovate them to live into new and modern expectations for children's ministries. Rural and suburban churches may be situated in open areas with room for expansion, but there may not be a population of children who could use expanded services.

The actual location of a church may also affect how it is in ministry for children, ranging from the influences in a very poor neighborhood, to location by a noisy and dangerous road, to the availability of a public park adjacent to the church. The implications of the ministry setting are many, and require advocates to understand the opportunities and threats of the setting they are in. A church in Illinois was thinking very seriously about adding child care to the ministries of the church. The demographic characteristics, that is, the increasing numbers of double-income families, the lack of other child care in the city, and the growing numbers of children under age six, indicated the need for infant care through after-school programs. A church-based child care ministry would provide an answer for many families and might serve as an entry point into the church. Further, it would ensure a safe place for children close to home.

Looking around the church building, the members decided that the basement classrooms would be an ideal place to house such a program. However, when they checked the state requirements for licensed child care, they learned they would have to provide an additional entrance into the basement, purchase the home next door and demolish it to provide outdoor play space, and upgrade their fire and smoke alarm systems. These were only three changes in a very long list of actions they would have to take in order to provide a child care ministry. Their church building's environment was not conducive to housing a child care ministry without huge expense.

A small church may feel that their resources are limited. After all, a church of few members still must pay for the heat and the air conditioning, the leaky roof, and the pastor's salary. Moving out into the world to make a difference for someone else's children may be a task they don't feel they can consider. Creating a nursery in the church that may attract younger people but will certainly care for the little ones seems like a very large task, but many churches have accomplished that goal. It is the work of the child advocate in the church to identify needs and lift them high so that they can be seen and understood by the congregation.

"SWOT" Analyses

In the examples above, persons considering advocacy ministries first utilized a technique of strategic planning called "SWOT" analysis. SWOT stands for Strengths, Weaknesses, Opportunities, and Threats. "Strengths" and "Weaknesses" are internal conditions that affect the potential success of current and future ministries of a church or agency. These conditions include current finances, the condition of the building or area of the building that will house the new ministry, the support and capabilities of current staff, existing resources for ministry, and more. "Opportunities" and "Threats" are forces outside of the church or agency, such as changing economic conditions, other buildings and organizations in the immediate area, traffic conditions, political climate, and funding realities. Looking at all of these together provides a clearer picture for planning. Consideration of strengths, weaknesses, opportunities, and threats allows an understanding of possibilities of the environment in which a church or agency is located. In addition, this kind of analysis helps in other aspects of ministry planning, such as financial planning.

Safe Sanctuaries

One of the places the Church has been in recent years in the area of advocating for children is called *Safe Sanctuaries*. According to the General Board of Discipleship:

> Safe Sanctuaries is more than guidelines, policies and procedures implemented to create an environment in which children, youth and the adults who work with them have boundaries of safe space. Safe Sanctuaries is an overt expression of a congregation in making a congregation a safe place where children and youth may experience the abiding love of God and fellowship within the community of faith.[4]

The Safe Sanctuary system developed and distributed across the denomination is, on the one hand, about creating safety for children and youth—physically, emotionally, and sexually—in our congregations. On the other hand, the church has also recognized that the faith development of children is at stake. Any abuse of children destroys trust, the heart of a child's growing faith.

In 1996, the General Conference of The United Methodist Church passed the first resolution calling for United Methodists to reduce the risk of child abuse in the church. It grew out of increasing awareness, concern, and publicity nationwide of cases of child abuse, both sexual and physical, occurring in our churches and in church-related ministries, such as camping. Litigation against churches over the next few years grew in numbers of cases and in the size of monetary settlements. Insurance companies became actively involved in working with churches to ensure safety in this area. The United Methodist general boards began to work earnestly toward equipping congregations with materials and guidelines for making each church a safer place for children.

The changes made in our procedures and policies in the faith community since the publication of guidelines and the efforts in resourcing local churches and others have made a big difference in the opportunities for safety of our children. And these changes are a form of advocacy—of taking action that makes a difference for children.

At the same time, the Safe Sanctuary movement was a place we never thought we'd have to go. The consistent reporting of abuse in the church has shaken and frightened us. It has been a long, hard road to acceptance that it *can* happen "here," in our own local churches and our own children's ministries. In our experience, many churches were and still are reluctant to make the decisions needed to implement "safe sanctuary" rules and procedures. It is hard work. It is a child advocate's work, and, if your church has not yet written, adopted, and implemented Safe Sanctuary policies and procedures, it is time to travel this road. It will make a difference in the lives of children.

In the World, through the Church

People can advocate through the church as a whole by taking action on behalf of children in the church and in the world so that children might live better lives. Simple examples are serving meals at the church or collecting school supplies for children, teaching children and adults about the needs of the children of the community, state, nation, or world, or helping church members understand the culture and traditions of immigrants in their communities. The Children's Fund for Christian Mission[5] is an example of one way persons can advocate through the church. This fund generates funding for a variety of child-focused ministries in the United States and around the world. It also provides an educational tool for teaching children about mission and giving (i.e., stewardship). The church is the venue for advocacy for children beyond the church in the world.

Another example of this is the recent endorsement of a resolution by a coalition called "Faith against Tobacco" by our United Methodist Men. They join the United Methodist Women, the General Board of Church and Society, and others in a group united against tobacco use by young people. The resolution calls for increasing the cost of tobacco products as an effective means of preventing use by youth. The United Methodist Men urges churches to become involved in its efforts, which it sees as a natural extension of their current work to protect children.[6]

Another means of advocating for children through the church is to participate in the National Observance of Children's Sabbath. Organized by the Children's Defense Fund[7] (CDF), a Children's Sabbath is an opportunity to honor the gifts of children, build awareness of children's issues, and witness to the need for justice and peace for children in the world. Traditionally held the third weekend in October, Children's Sabbath services in churches, synagogues, and mosques across the country lift the importance of making the world a better place for children. Some groups organize interfaith, community-wide celebrations or call-to-action gatherings.

Each year CDF distributes a comprehensive Children's Sabbath guide that contains resources for worship, study, and action in response to critical issues. These materials, developed for a wide range of religious traditions, can also be used throughout the year for worship services, individual devotions, or adult and child learning contexts. The guide also includes promotional materials, bulletin inserts, and lesson plans for all ages in religious educational settings. A Children's Sabbath is also a time when children of the congregation might be asked to lead prayer or read Scripture, particularly if they are not often in those roles.

Churches can, of course, observe a Children's Sabbath at any time of the year, but the third weekend of October is a strategic choice. Given its proximity to general elections on the first Tuesday of November, Children's Sabbath reminds people of faith to think about children's issues when they go to the polls to vote for national and state leaders.

In the World, through Agencies and Organizations

Agencies

Many organizations in our local communities and in the world serve children and youth. Some of these agencies are "connected" to annual conferences of The United Methodist Church by funding, charter, or covenant relationships. For example, four child-serving agencies—ChildServ, Marcy-Newberry Association, Rosecrance, and Methodist Youth Services—are affiliated with the Northern Illinois Conference. The churches of the conference support these agencies through their prayers, service opportunities, and financial gifts through a coalition of advocates called "United Voices for Children." Marcy-Newberry is also one of the agencies related to and supported by the Women's Division of the General Board of Global Ministries. Your area may also have one or more child-serving agencies related to the annual conference or the Women's Division.

Such agencies are clear avenues for service and donations and under-gird the work of the child advocate in the local church. The agencies explain their missions and programs to churches across the conference, and they educate local church members on the critical issues that impact children, youth, adults, families, and guardians. Through reciprocal relationships, the agencies give opportunities for mission to local congregations, while the churches give financial, volunteer, and donation support to the agencies. Funds to these agencies support services for children in need—of that there is no doubt—but the ongoing interactions between agencies and churches create resources for both organizations that go beyond their financial relationships. Involvement with child-serving agencies is one of the ways churches serve and advocate for vulnerable children and youth.

Rosecrance Health Network[8] in Rockford, Illinois provides residential and outpatient treatment for youth and adults struggling with addictions. The original residential campus sat adjacent to Christ United Methodist Church, and a number of youth attended worship services there on Sundays. Members of the congregation encouraged them to participate in worship as greeters, ushers, and readers. The youth also felt secure enough in the worship service to share some of their challenges through their prayer requests. Church members learned a lot about addictions and their impact on young people and families through those heartfelt requests. The campus has now moved to another location, but the congregation continues to hold the young people in their corporate prayers. The church also supports the agency through financial gifts and donations.

Marcy-Newberry[9] welcomes work teams from across the country to one or more of their fourteen program sites each summer. These teams of youth and adults make minor repairs, paint classrooms and apartments, clean up yards, organize teaching materials, read to young children, and accompany agency children and youth on special outings. Marcy-Newberry's programs and buildings benefit from the hard work and the donated supplies of these work teams, and the volunteers learn about the challenges of children, youth, families, and elderly adults who live in poverty. These volunteers also gain "up-close" experience about serving Christ and neighbor through a community-based health and welfare agency related to The United Methodist Church.

If there is no United Methodist-related agency in your area, take a look around. You'll find other worthy organizations that serve children and families. Every conference, county, and state has them. They represent places in which modern-day disciples and local churches can carry out their missions to touch the lives of vulnerable children with healing and hope.

Child advocates should find organizations like Rosecrance, Marcy-Newberry, or a Boys and Girls Club and get to know them and engage others in their work. Such relationships often compel us disciples to emulate the example of Jesus by going to places we never thought we would go. These new places offer us other opportunities of advocacy through volunteer projects, service on governing boards, or participation in advocacy initiatives.

Disaster Relief

In the light of ongoing world-changing disasters, child advocates will want to become familiar with the work of the United Methodist Committee on Relief (UMCOR).[10] Other church and secular agencies serving children and families after a disaster, such as the American Red Cross, are also extremely important. Children caught in natural or human-driven disasters have intense and immediate needs for survival and safety. Once the immediate crisis is past, these children have long-term needs of recovery and rehabilitation. Children, youth, and families on the Gulf Coast are living in an extended period of recovery and rehabilitation following the devastation of hurricanes in recent years. We think of the children in war-torn regions (e.g., Iraq and Afghanistan) and those who have survived tsunamis, floods, earthquakes, terrorist bombings, and more. UMCOR and other national relief organizations make it possible for advocates to mobilize people of faith to respond to the critical needs created by natural and human disasters.

UMCOR has facilitated the development and training of Crisis Response Teams in every annual conference of the United Methodist Church. These trained volunteers can respond quickly when a disaster strikes nearby, and they provide crucial linkages to local leaders and organizations when UMCOR staff and volunteers arrive on the scene. For persons farther away from the crisis, UMCOR issues special appeals for emergency relief funds from individuals and churches, and many churches ship school kits, health packets, and flood buckets to disaster areas under the direction of UMCOR.

This chapter has attempted to examine the "where" questions of child advocacy: where do we advocate for children, what are the various contexts for this important ministry? We can look at our world and divide it into a variety of areas for advocacy, but the reality is that all places are places for advocacy for children. There is no place where a child's needs can be ignored by persons of faith, persons who know that Jesus left his teaching ministry to go to the deathbed of Jairus' daughter and make her well. Places, with their unique characteristics, are foundational as vertical warp threads that create the structure of the fabric of child advocacy.

Questions for Reflection

1. Think about Bible stories that include children. What actions are taken in the story that demonstrate advocacy? Think about obvious overt actions that help children, as well as those that may be less obvious. For example, one way Jesus advocated for children in the feeding stories in the Gospels was obviously and overtly to feed them. But, in John's version[11] a child becomes important when Jesus uses the fish brought by a child to feed the people. Jesus lifts the child up as one who has gifts to share.

2. Are there other characters in the Bible who "changed course" or went a new direction to advocate for a child? Write or talk about these people and their stories. Do you think actions on behalf of a child changed their lives in any way?

3. Remember a time when you have changed your plans to help a child in need, in your family, your church, or in the world. Would you define that help as advocacy? How did it make a difference in that child's life?

4. Think about the children in your church. In what ways do you advocate for them? In what ways might you be discriminating against them, practicing ageism?

5. What does the word *hospitality* mean to your church? Is it only for adults, or is it practiced towards children as well?
6. How are children leaders in your church? How are your own children included as leaders? Can you think of new ways they might be involved in leadership?

Action Steps

1. Find a list of church-related organizations and agencies in your community or area. How is your church, or how are you, involved in supporting these? Make a list of seasonal ways you might be of help to them, ways you might advocate for these organizations. Choose one way to follow through on this immediately.
2. Choose one group that you might help through your church or on your own. Contact it for information, and begin to publicize the needs of that group (e.g., the Children's Fund for Christian Mission).
3. Find out who is available to speak to churches and neighborhood groups about their organization or agency, and invite them to speak to your group or other groups in your church.

Chapter 5 Notes

1. For additional information, see Mary Jane Pierce Norton, *Making God Real for a New Generation: Ministry with Millennials Born from 1982–1999* (Nashville: Discipleship Resources, 2003).
2. Sharon Jayson, "Generation Y Gets Involved," *USA Today*, October 24, 2006, p. 2D.
3. This new generation is called the Homeland Generation by William Strauss and Neil Howe. See their website "Generation Watch" at http://home.earthlink.net/~generationwatch/gw_background.html
4. Joy Thornburg Melton, *Safe Sanctuaries: Reducing the Risk of Abuse in the Church for Children and Youth* (Nashville: Discipleship Resources, 2008). Visit www.gbod.org/ministries/family/safe/default.html.

5. Children's Fund for Christian Mission, General Board of Discipleship, 877-899-2780, www.gbod@gbod.org.
6. "United Methodist Men Join the Effort to Reduce Teen Smoking," United Methodist News Service, Sept 18, 2006, www.umcom.org.
7. Obtain a Children's Sabbath handbook from the Children's Defense Fund, 25 E Street, NW, Washington, DC 20002, 202-628-8787, www.childrensdefense.org.
8. Rosecrance Health Network, 1601 University Drive, Rockford, IL 61107, 815-391-1000, www.rosecrance.org.
9. Marcy-Newberry Association, 1073 West Maxwell Street, Chicago, IL 60608, 312-829-7555, www.marcy-newberry.org.
10. United Methodist Committee On Relief, General Board of Global Ministries, the United Methodist Church, 475 Riverside Drive, Room 330, New York, NY 10115, 1-800-554-8583, http://gbgm-umc.org/umcor.
11. John 6:1–14

CHAPTER 6

Demanding Justice
for Children

⧏ Critical Issues ⧐

Story

One summer Sunday, Diane's local newspaper[1] featured two photos on
the opinion page. One was of a very thin boy, sitting in a cracked plas-
tic dishpan, gripping the edges and crying. To the right of the dishpan
was a person's foot. The child's head was smaller than that foot, and his
arms were bone thin, the skin on his face tight across bone. His hair was
thin and sparse on his little head. The text explained that he was waiting for his mother to bathe him at a medical center in Niger, the world's
second-poorest country.

In contrast, there was a photo from a hamburger-eating contest in
Wisconsin on the same page. It showed a man with puffed out cheeks and
an open mouth, stuffing in a huge burger, with the hands and burgers of

other contestants in the foreground of the picture. The caption indicated that this was one of several eating contests that had taken place that day. In another town, a "winner" consumed 35 bratwursts in ten minutes.

The eating contest picture gave a sharp contrast between those who have too much to eat and those who have too little. The picture of the starving child calls for action. This child's tears remind us of the harsh reality of children who live on the edge, children whose lives are in jeopardy because of the unequal distribution of the world's resources. This child's tears make us think about the long list of threats to the health and well-being of many of the world's children, including the 81 million who live in the wealthiest country of the world.

Scripture

There have always been serious threats to the lives of children. Jesus certainly met children whose lives were filled with pain and suffering. He encountered one of them—a spirit-possessed boy—when he returned from the place we call the Mount of Transfiguration.[2] A father had brought his sick son to the disciples for healing,[3] but they did not know what to do. Some scribes in the crowd were also at a loss. Instead of helping the boy, the disciples and scribes began to argue with one another. It seems likely that they were arguing about who should take responsibility for helping this child.

You can probably remember such an argument in your own family, congregation, or neighborhood association. We are quick to say, "Someone should do something," but we are not so quick to propose a solution or suggest a course of action. We may even blame the parents for the child's situation or illness. We are also likely to ignore the larger systemic forces that contribute to the overall plight of children.

The boy in the Mark passage does not speak. Or perhaps he did speak, but his words were not heard as the adult argument swirled around him. So it is for many of the children in our communities. We often do not hear their voices because our voices are louder and our conversations more important (we think!). Children tug at our sides, and we respond, "Just a minute . . . " or "Not right now . . . "

In this chapter, we have the opportunity to listen to the voices of children who live in different regions of the United States. We will visit their communities, get to know their families, and learn about the issues that affect their lives. These children have many distinctions, but they have one important commonality. They are among the children who live in poverty, and their experiences represent millions of children who live in similar circumstances across the country.

Definition of Poverty

In December 2006, the National Center on Children in Poverty released a report[4] that documents the growth in poverty among children during the five-year period, 2000 through 2004. Child poverty dropped to an all-time low of 12.1 million children in 2001 but had climbed again to 13.5 million by 2004. In other words, an additional 1.4 million children became members of this country's "new poor" during that five-year period.

"The New Poor: Regional Trends in Child Poverty Since 2000" points out that national statistics mask the economic realities found in various regions of the United States. For example, the national rise in child poverty from 2000 to 2004 was an 18 percent increase, but the Midwest generated 43 percent of that national rise in children living in poverty. The report examines regional differences in the family characteristics of children who have seen the greatest rise in poverty in recent years.

The United States defines poverty by using an outdated formula developed in the 1950s.[5] At that time, families spent about one-third of their income on food. Over fifty years later, the official poverty scale is still set by multiplying food costs by three, even though the average family in the early years of the 21st century spends far less than one-third of its income on food. Housing, child care, health care, and transportation costs now demand a disproportionate share of a family's income when compared to the cost of food.

The official poverty measure takes into account a variety of income sources, including earnings, interest, dividends, and benefits, such as Social Security and cash assistance. It does not, however, take into account the value of the major benefits that assist low-income families—the federal Earned Income Tax Credit, food stamps, Medicaid, child care subsidies, and housing assistance. On the expense side, the official poverty measure does not include the cost of payroll and income taxes or work-related expenses (i.e., child care and transportation). Calculations to set the federal poverty levels also do not include out-of-pocket medical expenses or regional differences in the cost of living.

In 2007 the federal poverty level was $20,650 for a family of four, but research consistently points out that most families need an income about twice the federal poverty level to make ends meet. Therefore, the National Center for Children in Poverty, along with other groups, defines families living between the two levels as low income. Thirty-nine percent of the nation's children—more than 28 million in 2007—live in low-income families.[6] Therefore, in the sections that follow, "poverty" refers to the federal poverty guidelines ($20,650 for a family of four), and "low-income" describes the families that live between the $20,650 (poverty level) and $41,000 (the level at which the average family of four "breaks even").

Midwest

Antoine lives in a medium-sized city in the heart of the Midwest. A 13-year-old, Antoine is doing an assignment on family occupations for his social studies class. Here's how he describes his parents and their jobs:

> My mom and dad both work. My dad drives a delivery truck, and my mom works as a nurse's assistant at a nursing home. We have one car, and my mom drives to work each day. It takes almost an hour to get to the nursing home, but that's not too bad. If she took the bus, it might take her up to two hours because she would have to transfer to two other buses to get from our neighborhood to the suburb where the nursing home is located. She has to work every other weekend, and she often works on holidays because she makes extra money on those days. I was really happy that she did not work on Christmas Day, but I could tell that she felt like she should have worked that day. My dad takes two buses to get to work. Once his truck is loaded at the warehouse, he spends the day deliv-

ering office supplies to stores on the south side of the city. Many of the boxes on the truck are very heavy, and yesterday's snowstorm made his job even harder. Traffic was very slow, and he had to work late to finish his deliveries. It was almost bedtime when he finally got home. He said he got tired of waiting for the second bus so he walked part of the way home rather than stand in the cold at the bus stop. He reminded Mom that the buses don't run as frequently since the funding for public transit was cut by the state.

Antoine knows that his parents' jobs involve long hours and physically demanding work. He also suspects that they worry about money. Their rent went up a lot just a few months ago, and a couple of nights ago Antoine heard his parents talking about the electric rates going up 12 percent the next month. His mother said, "Pretty soon we will need to move to a cheaper place or take the boys off the health insurance." His father responded, "It's going to be hard to find a decent apartment that costs less than the one where we live now." The family had moved from their previous apartment because a couple of children who lived in the building were diagnosed with lead poisoning.

Antoine's mom has health insurance through her job, but she has to pay for the rest of the family to be covered. She complains that the insurance rates go up every year and that last year the amount of the deductible went up as well. She worries that her husband will hurt his back with all the lifting he does on his job. Antoine doesn't get sick very often, but his brother, Lamont, has asthma and makes numerous trips to see the doctor. Antoine remembers when the family had no health insurance, and his parents took Lamont to an emergency room when he was ill. The ER doctor told his parents that the pollution from a nearby factory was making Lamont's asthma worse. Antoine has several friends who also have asthma and miss a lot of days of school because they are ill.

Antoine and Lamont hope the family does not have to move. Their apartment is small, and the landlord doesn't always take care of the building the way he should, but they have friends in the building, and it's not too far from their school. They usually walk to school, but sometimes they take the bus when the weather's bad or when there's been some trouble on the streets.

Antoine and Lamont represent many other children in the Midwest whose parents are working, but, nonetheless, have slipped into poverty over the past few years. Over half a million children (634,075)[7] more children were living in poor families, a 28 percent increase from 2.2 million in 2000 to 2.8 million in 2004. In this region, poverty rates rose the most among children with employed parents and among children whose parents did not have a college education. Antoine and Lamont's family reflects these two characteristics.

By 2004, 5.5 million children living in the Midwest had parents who had a high school education or less. Over one-third of these children (35%) were poor. Among children whose parents are working, whether full-time or part-time, the poverty rate increased by 2 percentage points, from 11% to 13% while poverty rates among children with nonworking parents declined by 1 percentage point from 73% to 72%.[8] In the Midwest, increases in child poverty during this period did not vary by the nativity status of the children's parents or children's race and ethnicity.

South

Maria lives in a small town in the middle of the South. She has lived in this community for almost two years, but she continues to feel like a stranger. She and her parents, along with her three brothers and a baby sister, moved here from the Southwest, but her family originally lived in northern Mexico. Maria misses her hometown. She especially misses her grandparents and her friends at her school. She longs to be in place where everyone looks like her and speaks her language. Every day she works hard to learn a little more of her new language, but at least once every day she groans to herself and says, "English is *muy difficil* (very hard)." She tries to ignore the unfriendly looks she gets when she makes mistakes or uses Spanish when she cannot remember the correct English word.

She hopes to return to her hometown one day, but she is old enough to realize that there were not enough jobs for all the people who had families to support. Her new home may feel strange to her, but at least her parents and older brother have found work. Her father works in a small factory during the week and clears tables in a restaurant three nights a week and on weekends. Her brother Jose works in the same restaurant after school every day. Her mother cleans houses while Maria and her siblings are in school.

An elderly neighbor, a substitute grandmother for the children, cares for the baby during the day. She doesn't charge very much, but Maria's parents still struggle to come up with the weekly fee. They also know that Abuela (grandmother) Garcia needs more than she is charging. She lives with her adult son who dropped out of school when he was fifteen. He does yard work and other odd jobs around town, but his wages are very low. Together, he and his elderly mother barely cover their modest living expenses. Neither of them receives any kind of public assistance or Social Security.

Maria's family lives in a small, somewhat dilapidated house on the edge of town. The rent is high, but they feel lucky to have the house. Maria's mother has planted a small vegetable garden in the side yard. Growing some of their own food helps keep the grocery bill down. Besides, the tomatoes taste wonderful, and her family likes sharing their bounty with the neighbors, especially Abuela Garcia. Maria would, however, be surprised if she knew that her parents spend more than one-third of their income to cover the rent for their house.[9]

Maria does not realize it, but families like hers experienced a 6 percent increase in poverty between 2000 and 2004, while there was a 1% increase in poverty among native-born families. Almost one-third (1.13 million) of children living with immigrant parents in the South are poor.[10] In recent years, several Southern states have had large influxes of immigrants with lower education levels and limited English proficiency. These immigrants have, in many cases, benefited local economies, but they tend to work in low-wage, service sector jobs without health insurance, unemployment benefits, and family/medical leave.

Overall, the South experienced a 10% increase in the number of children living in poor families, rising from 4.9 million in 2000 to nearly 5.4 million in 2004. Nearly one-half million more children (452,755) lived below the poverty line in the United States' 17 southern states in 2004 than five years before. Increases in child poverty did not vary by parents' employment or their education. Instead, parents' nativity status constituted a strong, determinant factor. Poverty among immigrants accounted for two-thirds of the increase in the number of children living below the poverty line. Since it is the region with the fastest growing immigrant population, the South is likely to see a continued increase in poverty over the next five to ten years.

Northeast

Jack and Matthew live near each other in a mid-sized city in the Northeast. They attend the same high school and participate in sports together both at school and at a city park during the summer. Their families know each other but do not socialize very often even though both families attend United Methodist churches. Matthew's family is active in a suburban Korean United Methodist congregation while Jack's family attends a predominantly white congregation near his home.

Jack and Matthew spend most Saturday afternoons together. This Saturday, in mid-July, they are at Matthew's house washing and waxing his family's car. Jack has just told Matthew that he does not expect to play football in the upcoming season. Matthew protests, "Come on, Jack, you know you don't mean that! You're crazy about football, and besides, the team needs you. You know that we're going to be short some players this year."

Jack shakes his head and says, "Look, Matt, you know my father's store is not doing well. It's a pretty small place, and his sales really dropped since the mega-store opened on the edge of town. People have to drive farther to get there, but the prices are better than Dad can offer. For a while people still came to the store because they stopped there to get gas, but now the mega-store has added a gas station. The gas costs a lot less at that station, and Dad thinks that's where his customers are going. The other night he said, 'I just can't compete with mega-store's prices.'"

Matthew responds, "Well, yeah, I guess I knew that things were tough at the store. It makes me mad! Your dad's store and gas station have been in this neighborhood for a long time. You'd think the people here would be more loyal! But maybe this is just temporary. Maybe things will get better before school starts."

Again, Jack shakes his head. "I hope you're right, Matthew, but I doubt it. Besides, that's not our only problem. My mom's been sick, and we have lots of medical bills since the insurance covered only a portion of the hospital bill. She's probably going to have to go back to the hospital, and we're just not going to have the money for me to play football this year. You know what the uniforms cost, and besides, I need to get a job if I can find one. I'll probably be working while you're at practice every afternoon."

The two boys talk about the problem as they finish up the two cars. Matthew keeps trying to figure out a solution, but Jack does not want to get his hopes up too high. He loves football, but, more important, he had hoped that he would play well enough this year to get a scholarship for college. He really wants to go to college, but now he feels like he has to face the possibility that he will have to drop out of school. If his mother's health does not improve, he will have to work even more hours. Since he just turned sixteen, he believes that he should contribute to the family's income.

Matthew finally urges Jack to talk to their coach. "He'll figure out something to help you with the uniform and stuff. You know how much he needs you on the team since Pete and Jim can't play this year because they were taking drugs last year. Coach will do something. I know he will." Jack shakes his head again. "I have to get a job now, Matt. I can't wait until after football season is over. My family needs my help now."

A few minutes later Jack heads for home. He walks home slowly, thinking about football and college. Matthew goes inside, feeling a little guilty. Somehow over these past three years, things have gotten better for his family while they've gotten worse for Jack's. Matthew wonders what makes things like that happen.

Jack and Matthew do not know much about the economic systems that affect their community and their families. They do not know that the Northeast experienced an 11% increase (205,144 more) in the number of children living in poverty between 2000 and 2004.[11] They also do not know that the increase of children living in poverty from 1.9 million in 2000 to 2.1 million in 2004 did not vary according to parents' employment, education, or nativity. The increase in child poverty in the

Northeast, instead, varies by race and ethnicity. White children were the only racial/ethnic group to experience a statistically significant increase in poverty while Asian children in the Northeast were the only group to experience a decline in poverty.

West

Juan, Ebony, Walid, and Anna are sophomores at Ward High School in a mid-sized city in a large western state. They see one another every day in Ms. Bailey's biology class. Some of their friends complain that she gives a lot of homework, but they like the class and think Ms. Bailey is a great teacher. They quickly realized that Ms. Bailey expected a lot of them. She urged them to enter the district science fair, and talked with them about getting ready for college.

The four friends put in a lot of after-school hours working on their projects. Ms. Bailey was often there to answer questions and make suggestions. She also paid for many of the supplies they needed. One afternoon, she created a "college bound" display while they were working.

Ebony asked, "Ms. Bailey, why are you always talking about our going to college? What's so special about college? My dad says it costs too much money for me to go."

Ms. Bailey responded, "It does cost a good bit of money to go to college, but there are scholarships, loans, and other types of financial aid that can assist any student who wants to go to college."

"But," Juan asked, "why does it matter so much whether we go to college or not? My folks didn't go to college. They say that kids in this town don't go to college."

Ms. Bailey said, "Some young people from this town, from this school even, go to college. I want you to go to college because you deserve to go. You're all smart, you work hard, and you'll have a better chance at a good job if you go to college."

"That's not true," interrupted Anna. "My dad went to college, and he just lost his job. Mom says that none of us kids is allowed to get sick because we don't have medical insurance now! I don't know what we're going to do if Dad doesn't find another job pretty soon. We won't have money for groceries, much less college!"

Ms. Bailey said, "I'm really sorry that this is a difficult time for your family, Anna." A few minutes later she suggested that it was time to stop for the day.

As they waited for a bus, Ebony said, "Ms. Bailey just doesn't understand. I can't go to college. My mom needs me to help with my brothers after school while she's working at the mall. Even if I got a scholarship, I still couldn't go. Who would take care of the kids? Mom can't afford an after-school program, not even the one at the church!"

Walid nodded. He knew that his family never had enough money to cover all their basic expenses. Suddenly they realized that they would not have time to do science projects next year. They would need to work to help with their families' expenses, that is, if they could find jobs.

Two weeks later, Ebony, Walid, Anna, and Juan traveled to a high school in a suburban community 15 miles away from their homes. The school looked brand new, and it was much larger than their school. The four friends were impressed by the state-of-the-art science classrooms and adjoining labs. The rooms had stainless steel tables, sinks, refrigerators, microscopes, scientific journals, and shelves filled with beakers and tools.

The next day the four students had a long conversation with Ms. Bailey. Juan finally asked the question that puzzled them the most. "Why does Sanders School have such great labs and all the latest equipment and our school doesn't?"

"Yeah," Ebony chimed in, "why can't we have stuff like that in our school?"

Ms. Bailey sighed and said, "First of all, please believe me when I say that the reason is not that the students at Sanders are smarter or better students than the students here at Ward. The inequity that you see is the result of the way we fund schools in this state."

Walid asked, "What do you mean? I heard a couple of men talking on the bus last week. One of them said, 'We pay all those taxes and still the teachers don't teach and the kids don't learn.'"

Anna said, "That's not true! Ms. Bailey is a great teacher, and we learn a lot from her. I bet we know much more than those two men do!"

Ms. Bailey smiled and said, "Thanks, Anna. I appreciate the vote of confidence. However, many taxpayers agree with their opinion."

Shaking her head, Ebony said, "If our schools are funded by tax dollars, I don't understand why Sanders has so much more money than Ward."

Ms. Bailey explained, "Schools are funded by several different sources,[12] including state income tax dollars, but state funding covers only about 25–45%of the cost of education. Federal funding adds about 7%, and the remainder is contributed by local communities, usually through property taxes levied by each school district. So a town with expensive housing has higher property taxes and raises more money for schools than a community like ours that has more modest housing. Each school district has a different amount of money to dedicate to its schools."

"So," Juan said slowly, "the state tax money is distriuted to each school district, but the property taxes are not the same across the state."

"That's right," said Ms Bailey. "Our district spends between $5,800 and $6,800 on each student, but Sander's district spends about $14,500. That's why Sanders School has more teachers and the science labs are so well equipped."

Poverty remains the single greatest deterrent to a child's opportunity to live a full and healthy life.

"It's not fair," fumed Ebony.

"You're right, Ebony, it's not fair," said Ms. Bailey. "A number of organizations across the state have proposed raising the state income tax in order to generate more money for schools, but many legislators are very reluctant to raise taxes, even though polls show that people are willing to accept increased taxes *if* the money goes to education."

Walid asked, "How can we say we live in a democracy if school funding is not equal? Isn't democracy about equal opportunity?"

In 2004, there were 3.2 million children living in poverty in the West. Unlike the other regions, there was no statistically significant increase in child poverty in this region between 2000 and 2004. Poverty levels dropped slightly among African American, Asian, and Latino children and remained the same among white children. The largest drop, from 13% to 9%, was, like the South and the Northeast, was among Asian children.[13]

In the West, the most racially diverse region in the United States, children of parents with less formal education were more likely to be poor, but during the years from 2000 to 2004, children whose parents had at least some college experienced greater increases in poverty. Anna knows that her father's job loss is very serious, but she does not realize that job losses, that is, unemployment, seems to have been more concentrated among those with higher education levels during the five-year period of the research carried out by the National Center for Children in Poverty.[14]

A Closer Look

The stories that you have just read give us glimpses of the real-life experiences of millions of children and youth who live in poor or low-income families in all regions of the United States. The names of the children and adults in the stories are not their real names, and their stories are composites, rather than being stories about specific individual children or families. Any resemblance to an individual or family that you know is coincidental.

It may be tempting to dismiss the difficult experiences and complex dilemmas of the families in these stories. Perhaps their circumstances do not seem dire enough to merit further attention. Perhaps some aspect of their struggles calls to mind an experience of your own or the experience of someone close to you. You may want to suggest that if the parents just work harder, the family situation will improve. The reality is that these parents are already working very hard—often at more than one job—but, in most cases, things do not get better. Their wages are very low, they have no health insurance, and their living expenses continue to rise. The parents struggle to make ends meet, and their families fall farther and farther behind their counterparts in middle-income and affluent communities.

Some experts contend that we have poor children and low-income families in this country because we tolerate—even accept—persistent child poverty.[15] Seventy-five years ago our national leaders made a collective decision, bolstered by substantial public opinion, to address poverty among the elderly. While it is not without its critics, the resulting Social Security system has had a positive impact on the quality of life for millions of older Americans. In spite of a significant effort in the War on Poverty of 1960s and 1970s,[16] we, as a nation, have not yet made a similar decision on behalf of children. Yet research shows that poverty remains the single greatest deterrent to a child's opportunity to live a full and healthy life.

Children and youth who live in poverty are more likely to go without regular health care, live in substandard housing, eat a high-carbohydrate, low-protein diet, and attend schools with reading scores well below grade level. Children who live in low-income, poor, and extremely poor families are also more likely to die before their first birthday, live with an undiagnosed learning disability, and lack access to dental care during the preschool years. Youth who live in low-income, poor, and extremely poor families are more likely to repeat at least one grade in school and drop out of high school before graduation.

These stories do not include the full range of issues that threaten the well-being of children and youth. With all their challenges, the above mentioned young people have not experienced directly the traumas of child abuse, war, famine, gun violence, sex-trade prostitution, illegal child-labor practices, life-threatening diseases, or the devastation of hurricanes and tsunamis. You can apply the advocacy principles and practices presented in this book to any child and family issue that you want to pursue. The appendixes include a list of advocacy organizations and websites that generate statistics, and other data related to a wide range of issues. We encourage you to do some basic research on one issue for which you have great concern and passion—and keep reading to learn more about organizing for justice and building a movement for children.

This chapter began with an argument between two groups of religious people who did not know what to do about a seriously ill child.

Jesus became very angry when he realized that the disciples have not helped the child. He said to the disciples, "You faithless generation, how much longer must I be among you? How much longer must I put up with you?" (Mark 9:19) Jesus was not talking to the scribes or other curious onlookers in the crowd. He was talking to the disciples! Jesus expected his disciples to take action, to do something for this suffering child, and he admonished them for their lack of action. Before we say, "Shame on those disciples," we should acknowledge that many of us reacted in much the same way to the story of the destitute child in the newspaper picture. We, too, often do not know what to do about children and families in crisis, but Jesus' response to the father and the disciples tells us that he expects us—his modern-day followers—to stop debating and take action.

We have added the critical issues that threaten the well-being of many children and the very survival of others as new threads on the warp of the loom. We have also brought our commitment to touch the lives of children with healing and hope and to change the conditions that prevent them from living whole and healthy lives. We have said that advocacy is not a single act; advocacy is a process, a way of life. The threads of the warp demonstrate the complexity of that process, but we accept this challenge from Jesus with gratitude as we work to change the conditions and systems that prevent children and youth from living whole and healthy lives.

Questions for Reflection

1. What are some ways that your church reaches out and touches children who are suffering? Is their pain due to physical illness or family circumstance? How many of these children are active participants in the congregation's worship and community life?

2. Spend a few minutes thinking about your reactions to the stories presented in this chapter. Identify those aspects of the stories that you found most disturbing. Next, identify those aspects that you see as signs of hope for these children, youth, and their families.

3. What similarities do you see between the children and youth in this chapter's stories and those you see and know in your own community? In your church? What differences do you see?

4. Spend some time thinking about the statement on page 108, "we have poor children and low-income families in this country because we tolerate—even accept—persistent child poverty." What evidence do you see in your community that leads you to believe that this statement is true? What evidence do you see when you survey the national scene as it relates to children in poverty?

Action Steps

1. Read Micah 6:8. Make three columns on a sheet of paper and put as headings over the columns: Love Kindness, Do Justice, and Walk Humbly with Your God. Then reread one of the regional stories about child poverty. Record ways that you as an individual child advocate can show kindness, do justice, and walk with God with and on behalf of the children in the story that you have chosen. Identify ways that your church can live out the mandates given to us by Micah for these children.

2. Learn more about the demographics of your own community along with the communities that surround yours. Are the incomes of most families fairly similar or are there substantial gaps between the income levels of the community's families? Do some research to learn more about the implications of those gaps. For example, determine whether the difference in income levels affects the per-pupil amount spent on education in the several communities that you have studied.

3. Do some research on the education funding formula in your state. Find out how much your school district invests in each student every year and compare that with the per-pupil spending in other nearby districts. Talk with a school

principal and a leader in the school's parent association to get their perspectives on school funding issues. Ask them to identify some local and statewide groups that advocate for additional school funding and/or other school reforms (e.g., restructuring the state tax structure in order to distribute school funding more equitably across the state). Organize a forum in your church to explore ways in which people of faith might get involved in advocating for a more just educational system in your state.

Chapter 6 Notes

1. *The Minneapolis Star and Tribune*, August 21, 2005.
2. Mark 9:2–13; also Matthew 17:1–8 and Luke 9:28–36.
3. Mark 9:14–29; also Matthew 17:14–21 and Luke 9:37–43a.
4. "The New Poor: Regional Trends in Child Poverty since 2000," Report from the National Center for Children in Poverty, Columbia University, Mailman School of Public Health, January 2006.
5. "'Who Are America's Poor Children?' The Official Story," Report from the National Center for Children in Poverty, Columbia University, Mailman School of Public Health, November 2007.
6. Ibid.
7. "The New Poor: Regional Trends in Child Poverty Since 2000," 4.
8. Ibid., 4–5.
9. "'Who Are American's Poor Children?' The Official Story," 3.
10. Ibid., 5.
11. "The New Poor: Regional Trends in Child Poverty since 2000," 6.
12. School funding formulas vary from state to state and are far more complicated than this discussion indicates. Each state's Board of Education provides detailed information about all sources of education funding and the formula by which the funds are allocated to individual school districts.
13. "The New Poor: Regional Trends in Child Poverty since 2000," 7.
14. Ibid., 7.
15. One compelling analysis is found in Lee Rainwater and Timothy M. Smeeding, *Poor Kids in a Rich Country: America's Children in Comparative Perspective* (New York: Russell Sage Foundation, 2005), which uses income data assembled by the Luxembourg Income Study. Using income data from a number of countries, Smeeding and Rainwater point out, among other important facts, that poor children in France, Germany, and the Nordic countries are six times more likely to escape poverty than their American counterparts. They also point out that fully one-third of children of single mothers in the United States today are not just

poor but extremely poor. Low-income single mothers in the United States work more hours than do single mothers in other wealthy nations, yet have higher poverty rates.

16. The War on Poverty called for by President Lyndon B. Johnson in his 1964 State of the Union Address to the nation.

CHAPTER 7

Putting Advocacy into Practice

⋞ Walk the Talk ⋟

Story

Several years ago Laura Dean led a workshop on advocacy at a leadership development conference. In preparation for the session, she posted ten cards around the room, each bearing one of the numerals from one to ten. Following a moment of prayer, she asked participants to stand by the number that best represented their knowledge and skill in advocacy. The numbers one through three indicated very little knowledge and skill; four through seven meant some; and eight to ten stood for a lot of experience in advocacy. The twenty-three members of the group did not hesitate. Fifteen persons positioned themselves in front of the numbers one, two, and three. Six individuals grouped themselves at the numbers four and five, two persons stood at number six.

After a moment of reflection, the group discussed the implications of their "body sculpture." A man in the group spoke up, "We talk about children a lot in the church, but we don't talk very much about advocacy."

Many of us may feel we have a lot in common with these workshop participants. We care deeply about children and youth, we have leadership skills, and we are active members of churches or civic organizations. But sometimes we do not feel confident when it comes to organizing advocacy initiatives within the church, or we may want some fresh ideas to energize our child advocacy work. Whether you are a new or long-term advocate, this chapter will be of great help to advocates of all experience levels.

Scripture

It might be helpful to remember that Jesus—as an adult—also had to learn about advocacy, and he learned it, partially at least, through a most unexpected encounter. A Canaanite woman came to Jesus for help. Matthew 15:21–28 tells us that this woman interrupted Jesus and his disciples when they were relaxing away from the crowds that always gathered around Jesus. She was a foreigner, and she was unaccompanied by a husband or father. She was probably poor, perhaps a single mother and, by some standards, had crossed cultural and gender boundaries. She put herself in a very uncomfortable situation.

When we read that she spoke loudly to Jesus, we must recognize her courage. She was being assertive in a time when women did not speak to men outside their families. Her daughter was gravely ill, and this woman knew that Jesus could heal her. Jesus ignored her at first, and she turned to the disciples for help. They asked Jesus to get rid of her, but she did not leave.

An argument ensued, and Jesus made it clear that he did not come for people like her. He actually insulted her by saying that it was not fair to take the children's bread and give it to the dogs. "Dog" was a derogatory term that Jews used for Canaanite persons. But the woman held on to her conviction that Jesus could help. She put her daughter's interest ahead of hers and said, "Yes, Lord, but even the dogs gather the crumbs under the master's table." Her faith and persistence were persuasive! Jesus changed his mind and healed the daughter.

Essential Data and Resources

Laura Dean remembers the day Jane asked, "Is it possible for a church to help prevent child abuse?" The night before, her pastor had told the church council that their town had a higher number of calls to the child abuse hotline than the rest of the county. Jane and other council members had a long discussion that night. Eventually, the question changed from, "How can this be?" to "What should we do?" The church members did not believe that they knew enough about child abuse to make a difference, but they heard God's call to reach out to vulnerable children and families. They began with prayer, then studied and learned about child abuse and conducted a series of interviews with service providers in the community. Over time, the congregation developed a sustained ministry in child abuse prevention. The answer to their original question was, "Yes!"

Regardless of your level of advocacy experience, an important first step is gathering information about critical child and family issues. Knowledge is a powerful force for child advocates, and the information and data needed to build that knowledge are readily available from several important national and international child advocacy organizations. See Appendix B for a comprehensive list of important child advocacy organizations.

Most states also have a variety of organizations that amass statistics and other information about the well-being of children in communities across the state. For example, Voices for Illinois Children[1] publishes data on the impact of the state's budget and tax structure on the well-being of the state's children. "Raising voices to make every kid count," the Wisconsin Council on Children and Families promotes the effective and efficient health, education, and human service delivery for children and families across the state through citizen action. Its website[2] includes, among other important resources, an advocacy tool kit. Its board is made up of a wide range of professionals and concerned citizens, including a retired United Methodist bishop.

Take a look around, and you will probably find a similar advocacy organization in your town, county, or state. Other sources of information about child well-being, particularly those in your local community, include the United Way, the school districts, social service agencies, as well as your community's village trustees or City Council. Many municipalities, large and small, use census data to analyze child and family trends, and their reports are available to the general public. You can obtain data from local groups through personal phone calls, face-to-face meetings, or attendance at a village board meeting or a community forum.

Statistics often feel overwhelming, but this is a very important step. Take some time with the data, looking at trends over time and recent changes. Ask questions of persons who serve in the agencies from which you have obtained the data. As your knowledge increases, you will have information to support your advocacy efforts.

Organizing an Effective Child Advocacy Program in the Church

Principles

Diana Garland, the dean of the School of Social Work at Baylor University in Waco, Texas, outlines some important ingredients for effective advocacy in her book, *Precious in His Sight: A Guide to Child Advocacy*.[3] She stipulates that effective advocates:

- *Propose solutions to the problems being addressed.* Pointing out problems rarely results in change. Organizing a group of parents, church leaders, and other advocates to brainstorm and plan strategies for making a difference is far more effective. Rank the list of potential solutions by level of difficulty or interests of the group and then choose one or two "proposals" with which to move forward. The resulting changes may appear to be minor, but they are a beginning. They lay the groundwork for further changes and improvements.
- *Propose solutions that empower children and families to make decisions about their own lives.* Trusting parents and

guardians to make good decisions about their children is a crucial aspect of effective advocacy. The advocate's job is to support parents in their roles and to avoid strategies that make parents feel inadequate and frustrated. Getting to know parents, listening to their concerns, and thinking about issues from their perspectives will produce new ideas and new ways of working together.

- *Develop partnerships inside the human systems they are trying to influence.* Building relationships with school teachers and principals, the town's trustees, or health care professionals increases the church's knowledge of child and family issues and also creates opportunities for working with other groups on important community issues. Some towns and cities have coalitions organized around specific issues (e.g., public education, youth development), and the perspectives and resources of churches and other faith communities make an important contribution to those efforts. Collaboration with clergy groups or community organizations is another way to build partnerships.

- *Use more than one approach.* Developing a range of strategies for pursuing advocacy goals increases the likelihood of success. "Thinking outside the box" may be an over-used term these days, but it is a useful tool in this situation. There are always different ways to accomplish goals, and moving beyond "tried and true" can often produce a positive outcome. Involving a diverse group of people in the project's planning and implementation will produce more creative ideas and suggest new ways of working together.

Laura Dean's small, urban church wanted to develop a child care program for working families, but the building did not meet licensing requirements. Instead of feeling defeated, the outreach committee found another way to become involved in child care ministry. The church offered its building to a group of family child care providers to bring the children in their care for a morning of active play, messy art projects, and other activities difficult to provide in a home setting.

Planning

Garland's principles provide a good foundation for an effective advocacy program for your local church or for a community group of which you are a member. The following eight steps offer a comprehensive planning process to reach that goal:

1. *Acknowledge Abundance.* Recognizing that most of us have enough is an important place to begin. In our personal lives and in our churches, we usually operate out of a sense of scarcity, when, in fact, we live in the midst of abundance. Addressing issues of poverty and suffering is often a matter of allocation and distribution, not supply. We have plenty— more than enough, in many situations—but we find it hard to share, particularly with those who live in different communities and cultures. "Put your money where your mission is" was a popular saying a few years ago, but it bears thinking in this context as well. We need to consider carefully the balance between what our churches spend on congregational activities and what we invest in others.

2. *Infuse Theology.* Throughout this book, we have emphasized the critical role of theology in the important work of weaving a just future for all children. Our theology—love of God and neighbor—constitutes the loom with which we do our weaving. Many organizations provide good services as well as advocacy for children, youth, and families, but as faithful disciples, our understanding of who God is and how Christ calls us, defines our discipleship, and shapes our advocacy.

   We follow Christ's example—and that of John Wesley—when we understand that personal belief and social action are an interwoven aspect of living our faith in the world. Some strategies for infusing theology into our advocacy efforts include:

   • Pray for this ministry of advocacy and ask others to pray with you

- Organize a Bible study on children's issues or a Lenten study focusing on issues of children and poverty[4] or a sermon series on the biblical call to justice and mercy
- Participate in an interfaith witness for children (e.g., a community-wide Children's Sabbath service, candlelight prayer vigil, march against handguns)
- Wear religious symbols—a cross, ichthus (fish) or clerical collar—when meeting with legislators, participating in a community forum, or going to court
- Identify yourself as a person of faith when speaking with or writing a message to your legislators.

3. *Identify Obstacles.* Analyzing the congregation's approach to planning and decision making is an important step since some churches welcome new initiatives, but others approach such ventures with caution or reluctance. Consider as well the potential reactions that congregational leaders might have. Some typical objections include:

- "There's really nothing we can do to stop child abuse. We should leave that issue to the professionals."
- "Our church is already doing a lot in the community. We don't have time for any more activities, no matter how worthy they are."
- "We need to take care of our own children first."
- "We don't have the funds to start a new program or initiative."

These are legitimate concerns! Rather than dismissing these issues, we must take them into account as we develop advocacy initiatives. All human organizations, including the church, encompass a wide range of opinions, and we must learn to listen and talk with persons whose ideas or beliefs differ from ours. Too often, we are tempted to dismiss their objections without any exploration, but unresolved issues can undermine the important work we are doing. Identifying the areas on which we agree—children's health, for example—and then discussing the issues on which we have different opinions can help us find common ground and build new relationships. This takes time, of course, but developing consensus increases the potential for advocacy work in and through the congregation.

Other objections may emerge when church members discuss public policy issues. See chapter 8 for a more in-depth discussion of those obstacles.

4. *Engage Allies.* Getting others involved in developing an advocacy program is also very important. You might start by making a list of the "natural" allies (e.g., the Church and Society or Mission and Outreach committees in the congregation) along with individuals with commitment to justice and activism. Share information with them about your proposal for increasing the church's involvement in advocacy, invite them to join your effort, and ask them to suggest other persons who might participate.

Another important strategy involves searching for individuals or groups with concerns and interests that might intersect with yours. Libraries overwhelmed with school-age children every afternoon might join a coalition committed to developing new after-school resources for children in the community. Groups concerned about school readiness or children's health issues often collaborate with groups advocating for expansion of child care services for working families. These groups may not agree with every point of your plan. Therefore, work to identify common ground, acknowledge differences, build consensus, and forge partnerships with these community groups.

5. *Develop Structure.* Finding a place within the life of the church to "house" your advocacy efforts will increase your church's chances of success. Talk with members of one or more of the standing committees in your local church

(e.g., the women's group, the Mission Committee) about adding advocacy to the agenda of the group. Or, organize a new task force or committee by recruiting persons with passion and experience in working with or advocating for children. Include some of the persons whom you identified as allies, and reach out to some of the individuals who raised objections to the work (or issue) on which you have embarked.

Identify potential leaders and give them opportunities to lead and facilitate the work of the group. A skilled team of leaders creates a powerful force that sustains the work over time. Therefore, share your knowledge, support their efforts, and affirm their accomplishments. And, above all, be consistent about training all the volunteers—leaders and group members—in program development principles, advocacy strategies and public policy techniques.

6. *Build Plan.* Prioritizing the issues that members want to address is essential in order to channel your time and energy effectively. Recognize that you, your work group, and your congregation cannot focus on all the critical issues that affect the well-being of children. Consider the resources that you have—experience, interest, passion, skills—and make a thoughtful decision about the best way(s) to engage those resources. It may be helpful to review the different types of advocacy discussed on p. 68 in chapter 4 as you begin the planning process. And, of course, be open to the Holy Spirit's guidance throughout this phase of your work!

Make a decision about the initial focus of your group's advocacy and expect that other advocacy initiatives will grow from that first effort. God might call you to one of these areas of advocacy:

- one child—a child with a disability who cannot come to church
- small group—children who need help with reading

- particular issue—child care for low-income parents
- specific type—education (raising awareness) or public policy (legislative).

We know how to plan. We have done this work many times in our churches, businesses, and civic organizations. Applying our previous experience, we establish goals, objectives, and action steps along with tasks, timelines, and assignments. Building the plan will help clarify the group's priorities, but you may have to remind your coworkers that no church or committee or individual can do everything that needs to be done with and on behalf of children. In every community or church, there are other committed individuals and groups who are also working to make life better for children, youth, and families. Acknowledge their contributions to the overall work, and plan your efforts to complement theirs.

7. *Foster Action.* Putting the plan into action is a substantial challenge. These days, everyone is busy. Everyone has a heavily committed schedule. Therefore, the most effective plans are those with clearly articulated goals, action steps, timelines, and assignments. With those commitments in place, advocates—disciples—can move forward with their responsibilities. Everyone involved should emerge from the planning phase with two specific assignments: first, to pray, and second, to carry out a specific task. Some possibilities include:

- Write advocacy articles (or meditations) for the newsletter
- Recruit other volunteers to join the new initiative
- Attend public meetings related to child and family issues
- Speak out on legislation important to children
- Organize persons to make phone calls to the state legislature or Congress
- Plan an advocacy training session for people in the congregation.

Providing support to the workers is a crucial aspect of implementing the advocacy plan. Someone in the group—perhaps you—should accept responsibility for checking in with group members on a regular basis to see how they are doing and what issues or questions have arisen through their efforts. E-mail messages and phone calls are invaluable ways of staying in touch, reminding persons of their commitments, and encouraging them in their tasks.

8. *Evaluate Results.* Finally, as with any action plan, evaluation is crucial. We must identify and learn from our shortfalls, celebrate our accomplishments, and make adjustments in our strategy as we gain new insights or see new opportunities. Thoughtful and regular evaluation can make a significant contribution to our efforts to "grow the movement" for children, youth, and families.

We also build our advocacy capacity by recognizing the good work that's being done, celebrating the accomplishments of our colleagues, and telling the story of our commitment to children throughout the church. In addition, we should recruit and welcome newcomers to the work and forge new alliances both within the congregation and in the wider community.

Advocacy as Power

At a Christian Educators' Fellowship meeting during the Focus 2005 National Conference on Children's Ministries sponsored by the General Board of Discipleship, Laura Dean asked the participants to list words that describe advocacy. The answers came quickly—pray, intervene, care, stand, vote, organize, act, love, mediate, promote, change, and protect were among the suggestions. However, the answer that resonated most strongly across the room was "Speak truth to power."

Let's be clear: advocacy is about power. It's about the power that decision-makers have about resources, policies, procedures, allocations, and regulations. It's also about the power of people, individually and corporately, to ask questions and to challenge the status quo. It's about using that power to promote positive change for children, youth, and families, especially those who live in poverty.

Let's be clear: advocacy is about power.

Many children need an advocate with the courage and persistence of the Canaanite woman. She went to the place where power was, and she persisted even though she was ignored, pushed away, and called a name. She stood her ground and argued with Jesus, and insisted that her daughter had a right to be whole and well. Through her faith and conviction, she convinced Jesus to change his mind. Now, 2,000 years later and halfway across the globe, this nameless Canaanite woman stands as a model of a child advocate *par excellence*. She spoke "truth to power" and brought healing to her daughter's tortured life.

We have placed the last of the warp threads on the loom: the Canaanite mother's courage in the face of significant risk, her persistence in response to rejection, and her skills in debating with power. As we move into Section III—Discipleship and Vocation, our weaving will take shape as we bring the weft to the loom and the warp. Combining our spiritual insights and practical strategies with our understanding of discipleship and vocation will create a power-filled weaving that will inspire us to keep working for the day when all God's children receive healing and justice.

Questions for Reflection

1. Think about a situation in which you have seen a "Canaanite" woman (or man) advocating for a child or a group of children in an unreceptive or hostile environment. How did she or he convince others to pay attention or to

take action? What strategies can you adapt from that experience to use in current advocacy-needed situations?

2. Read Luke 2:40 several times. Think about the ways you see that kind of development in a child with whom you are close (e.g., your own child, a grandchild, a child in your congregation). Then think about parents and children that you do not know, who live in a different part of town, and pray that they will also have that kind of positive development for their children.

3. Focus your prayer and meditation time on Diana Garland's second ingredient (See pp. 116–117). Using your own experience as a parent, grandparent, or guardian, think about a time when a friend, colleague, or pastor's attempt to help with a child or family issue made you feel inadequate. Make a list of what they might have done differently that could have been helpful without diminishing your confidence or parental strategies. Use your list as a guide when you are working on child and family advocacy issues.

Action Steps

1. Review your notes from the community exercises suggested at the end of chapter 3 on pp. 60–61. Supplement your knowledge by reviewing some of the demographic data generated by groups in your local community. Refer to appendix B for a list of organizations that you might contact. Research a specific issue that's important to your community (i.e., public education) and focus your efforts in that area. Share your findings with others in the church through newsletter articles, discussions at committee meetings, or a sermon series.

2. Increase your skills by attending an advocacy conference in your state or annual conference. Network with other attendees and identify resources that will strengthen your advocacy capacity. Use your expanded skills and knowledge to plan an advocacy training session in your local

church. Consider attending the Samuel DeWitt Proctor Institute for Child Advocacy Ministry sponsored by the Children's Defense Fund every summer at the Alex Haley Farm in Clinton, Tennessee. See p. 159 in chapter 10 for more information.

3. Organize volunteer projects that engage children, youth, and adults in mission and outreach beyond the local church (i.e., working at a food pantry, cooking and serving dinner at a shelter, holding a holiday party at a nearby children's agency with funds raised by the children and youth of your church, volunteering to read to preschoolers at a child care program in a low-income community). Be sure to include some time for sharing and reflection after the experience.

Chapter 7 Notes

1. See www.voices4kids.org for more information. Voices for Illinois Children, 208 South LaSalle, Suite 1490, Chicago, IL 60604, 312-456-0600.
2. Go to www.wccf.org to download the Advocacy Tool Kit or write to Wisconsin Council on Children and Families, Inc., 555 West Washington Avenue, Suite 200, Madison, WI 53703.
3. Diana Garland, *Precious in His Sight: A Guide to Child Advocacy*, 2nd ed. (Birmingham: New Hope, 1996), 146–149. Garland cites research by Sheryl Dicker, published in *Stepping Stones: Successful Advocacy for Children*, (New York: The Foundation for Child Development, 1990), as basis for ingredients of effective advocacy.
4. *Community with Children and the Poor: A Guide for Congregational Study* is an excellent resource for local church study and action. It is available from Cokesbury in Nashville, Tennessee at 1-800-672-1789 or www.cokesbury.com, item #516543.

PART III: THE WEFT

Discipleship and Vocation

CHAPTER 8

Facing Facts

≷ Public Policy Matters ≷

Story

In 2006, along with legislators, teachers, principals, early childhood professionals, advocates, parents, and members of the press, Laura Dean witnessed the signing of the newly passed Preschool for All legislation. The room was electric with excitement. Illinois was the first state to establish free, developmentally-appropriate early childhood education programs for all three- and four-year-olds whose parents want this service for their young children. The bill mandated priority for children at risk of academic failure and also included funding for infant-toddler programs.

A group of four-year-olds and their two teachers were playing in the play space created by the concentric circles of chairs for dignitaries and parents. Engrossed in their play with Legos®, puzzles, dolls, and books, the children paid little attention to the proceedings until the governor invited them to come forward. They swarmed around the table and listened intently as the governor spoke with them briefly and watched as he signed the bill. Eyes shining, they clapped their hands as the audience rose for a standing ovation.

The governor indicated that he would take a few questions from the audience. This was the moment the press had been waiting for, but they did not seem interested in children or Preschool for All. Their questions focused on other policy issues in the state. The members of the press ignored the children, parents, and early childhood advocates in the room. How often this happens! When children are at the heart of the matter, the conversation often shifts to other "more important" issues.

Scripture

The prophet Micah presents a different view. He poses the question, "With what shall I come before the Lord, and bow myself before God on high?" (Micah 6:6a) He then goes on to say that God does not desire dramatic expressions of devotion and penitence (e.g., burnt offerings). Instead, Micah proclaims, "[God] has showed you, O mortal, what is good; and what does the Lord require of you but to do justice, and to love kindness, and to walk humbly with your God?" (Micah 6:6–8)

Many of us in the church define discipleship primarily in terms of personal faith and good deeds. Yet Micah exhorts people of faith to perform acts of mercy and, at the same time, to work for justice. When the disciples argued about who among them was the greatest, Jesus brought a child into their circle and said, "Whoever welcomes one such child in my name welcomes me . . . " (Mark 9:37a) He taught his disciples to touch, heal, and bless children and their families, and he calls upon his modern-day disciples to carry out those mandates in our churches, communities, and the world.

Other Imperatives

Our Wesleyan heritage also calls United Methodists to the task of integrating justice, kindness, and humility, which Micah demands of the faithful. Our Social Principles require specific attention and action on behalf of all children and youth, especially those who are vulnerable, in pain, alone, lost, or otherwise marginalized. Still, *advocacy* is not a word heard frequently in our local churches, and discussions of public policy issues are rare.

The legislative work of local, state, and federal governments often feels remote to the average citizen, and yet democracy demands an informed and participatory electorate. Every day decisions are made, policies developed, and laws enacted that either create new opportunities for our children, youth, and families or put stumbling blocks in their way. These public policy decisions do not happen in a vacuum. A complex interaction of personal attitudes, public opinion, and political aspirations fuels these legislative debates and budgets. This synthesis has a profound impact on the lives of our youngest people and their families all across the country.

Therefore, the imperative for Christians and other people of faith is clear: children and youth need our voices, our actions, and our votes to speak and act on their behalf. Our children and youth need people of faith to consider the full moral and ethical implications of the policies and laws that legislators consider and enact or defeat.

Children and youth need our voices, our actions, and our votes to speak and act on their behalf.

Many churchgoers express great concern for those who live in need nearby and far away, and they give special offerings, put together school kits, and donate food to local pantries on a regular basis. While acts of charity—good deeds—come naturally, it seems that, acts for justice occur less frequently. These same people of faith often demonstrate a reluctance to get involved in the legislative process or address community issues, such as housing, education, health care, hunger, safety, or taxes. Church leaders and members often treat the symptoms (i.e., tutor a child in reading) rather than acting on the hard questions, like, "Why are there so many children in our school who do not read well?" "What can we do to make education funding more equitable across the state?" Those questions encompass a complex mix of public opinion, legislative policy, and community practice. They are also at the heart of Christian discipleship.

Separate Domains

Local churches encourage their members to engage in a variety of spiritual disciplines and discipleship commitments. These endeavors rarely include involvement in public policy initiatives, particularly those that are being debated beyond their immediate communities. As a result, many people of faith do not make connections between their religious beliefs and their involvement in their civic lives (e.g., community and legislative affairs). They view discipleship and citizenship as separate domains. They may form opinions and make decisions about community debates and legislative matters with limited reflection on their faith.

The Micah 6:8 passage calls people of faith to "do justice and love kindness," but the prophet goes a step further and proclaims that the faithful must also "walk humbly with your God." (Micah 6:8b) In other words, our acts of kindness and our work for justice are to be carried out as spiritual disciplines. This spiritual discipline—listening to the voice of God—requires that we examine, individually and corporately, our long-held beliefs and practices in matters of faith and discipleship. This spiritual discipline—walking humbly with God—means that we examine all public policies and community developments in light of our Christian faith.

Quoting the prophet Isaiah, Jesus declared, "The Spirit of the Lord is upon me, because he has anointed me to bring good news to the poor. He has sent me to proclaim release to the captives and recovery of sight to the blind, to let the oppressed go free, to proclaim the year of the Lord's favor." (Luke 4:18–19) Jesus' good news addresses the maladies and systems that constrain human beings and offers, instead, opportunities for growth and freedom.

For those of us who are United Methodists, we need only to look at John Wesley's life and ministry to see the interconnectedness of individual (private) faith and social (public) action. Wesley preached personal salvation to people of all stations across England and at the same time, set up sewing cooperatives for poor women, established schools for children living in poverty, and visited men and women in prison for non-payment of debts.[1]

Congregational Approaches to Public Policy

Some denominations, including United Methodist, American Baptist, United Church of Christ, Episcopal, African Methodist Episcopal, and Presbyterian, charge particular boards or divisions with analysis and action on public policy matters as an integral aspect of their daily operations. Most of these denominations also have comparable regional, conference, or local groups that monitor and act upon public policy issues.

The General Board of Church and Society and the Women's Division of the General Board of Global Ministries of The United Methodist Church, for example, pay particular attention to federal legislation that impacts the poor (e.g., the minimum wage, immigration, criminal justice, education, welfare reform). These two groups educate others across the denomination through newsletters, action alerts, and website articles, but many members of local churches pay little attention to the information these groups provide to the church members across the denomination.

Protestants for the Common Good (PCG),[2] a faith and advocacy organization in Chicago, has worked over the past twelve years to assist people of faith to examine and exercise their citizenship in light of their Christian faith. PCG believes that churches are essential places to explore the faith dimension of political issues. Through its relationship with churches, PCG has identified three approaches that churches tend to embrace as their understanding of the church's role in public life (e.g., public policy engagement).

1. **The Silent Church**[3] is the congregation that does not
    involve its membership in public policy issues. This church

leaves direct political activity to the discretion of individual members, and, in some cases, the church may actually discourage members for taking action in the public arena.

The congregation assumes this stance over time for a variety of reasons, among them:

- Lack of interest in public policy issues
- Negative view of elected officials and the political process
- Fear that open discussion of public policy or politics increases conflict and division in the church
- Limited knowledge about ways that congregations can foster political activism.

2. **The Vocal Church**[4] describes the congregation that exhibits strong concern for the welfare of its community and acts on public issues, particularly on local matters, related to the quality of life of its citizens. The defining characteristic of the vocal congregation is that in response to community or public issues, the church takes a position on a specific piece of legislation, but rarely considers a wider range of public policy issues.

Some examples of the vocal church's approach include:

- Concern about families living in poverty gives rise to a support of an increase in the minimum wage
- Interest in local schools translates into advocacy for a bill that reduces class size or modifies the use of standardized tests.

3. **The Spirited Church**[5] asserts that involvement in social issues or political activism is a means of Christian witness. This church believes that it is important for congregations to promote active involvement in legislative issues and community life. This church rarely takes positions *as a congregation* on specific legislation and policies. Instead, it challenges church members and others to consider

community issues and public policy initiatives in the context of their Christian beliefs and practices.

Sometimes, the Spirited Church organizes a social policy group (e.g., Faith and Public Life), or designates one of its standing committees (e.g., Mission and Outreach), to focus on advocacy and public policy issues. This church may also interact with the social action arm of the denomination (e.g., the General Board of Church and Society of the United Methodist Church) or a secular advocacy organization (e.g., the Children's Defense Fund). Typical activities for a Spirited Church include:

- Education on the root causes of poverty and the public policy changes needed to help families become self-sufficient
- Development of a plan to build relationships between church members and their elected officials
- Initiation of voter registration and get-out-the-vote efforts.

Barriers

Church members often express reluctance to discuss or address public policy issues in their congregations. They make these comments:

- "Getting the church involved in legislative matters violates the separation of church and state."
- "Taking a stand on public policy issues will endanger our tax-exempt status."
- "Talking about politics at church will just cause a lot of hard feelings."

Church-State Issues

The beginning of the First Amendment of the Constitution states, "Congress shall make no law respecting an establishment of religion, or prohibiting the free exercise thereof." The First Amendment does not say that churches and religious groups cannot talk about matters of state (i.e., public life). Instead, the First Amendment declares that the Constitution prohibits any law being passed that establishes or denies the establishment of a specific religion or faith community. Further, the amendment requires that no law be passed to prohibit the free exercise of an individual's religion, nor can a law require a particular religious perspective or practice.

A law does not establish a religion if the law is supported by many religious people or even when most of its support comes from the individuals of a particular faith community. In other words, there is a difference between a law that has support from people of faith and a law that supports a specific religion or favors a particular religious practice. People of faith, then, are free to support or oppose whatever laws or policies they believe their faith requires of them.[6]

Tax Exempt Status

Churches are almost without exception defined as nonprofit, tax-exempt organizations under Part (c) of Section 501 of the Internal Revenue Service (IRS) Code. Discussing public policy issues in the church does not break any rules of the IRS. Churches can even participate in the political process to a limited extent without violating their tax-exempt status as long as their involvement is nonpartisan. For example, many churches across the country are used as polling places for elections. Churches can organize voter registration drives without any threat to their tax-exempt status as long as the drive is nonpartisan and does not endorse a particular candidate or political party. A religious congregation can also host a forum of political candidates as long as the church invites all candidates to speak and refrains from endorsing a specific candidate for political office.

Tax laws are complex, and it is appropriate, even advisable, for churches and other religious congregations to obtain legal opinion on questions related to their tax-exempt status.[7] Such consultation may help church members make decisions about joining or organizing a coalition to address a particular public-policy initiative (e.g., increased funding for public education).

Conflict

Conflict is a normal aspect of human organizations, including churches, but conflict makes many of us uncomfortable. Most of us look to our churches as places in which we find acceptance, approval, and companionship. We become uneasy when someone in the congregation—the pastor, the president of the women's group, the chair of faith and public life—introduces a controversial subject.

Each of us has probably known or heard about a church member or several members who left the congregation because the church sponsored a discussion about one of the "hot-button" issues of the day. We are often reluctant to discuss complex social issues because we know that a church leader or a personal friend—or, indeed, we ourselves—will become angry. We fear that we'll lose a friend if we disagree with that individual on capital punishment, gambling, or a vote by local workers to join a union. We want the church to be a place of harmony and refuge in a world characterized, all too often, by discord and fear. We want other people to like us, not be angry with us!

Conflict and anger can disrupt the life of a congregation; therefore, church leaders—lay and clergy—must develop a strategy for addressing those realities when they arise (or erupt!). A mutually agreed upon set of ground rules for discussion and deliberation can reduce conflict and enhance the debate on public policy issues. Training in conflict resolution can also be extremely helpful, particularly if a cross-section of church leaders and members learn those techniques and commit to putting them into practice in life of the congregation. The JUSTPEACE Center for Mediation and Conflict Transformation[8] produces resources, a newsletter, and training events to assist local congregations to deal with conflict in constructive, productive ways.

Strategies

Strong advocacy depends on several things: information, analysis, commitment, skills, tools, and people. Once we know what is happening in a particular area of concern—health care for uninsured children, for example—then we must share that information with others, recruit them to take action and then train and nurture them to become leaders who recruit others to take action. We recognize that people are busy and have limited time even when they care deeply about a particular issue. Therefore, we offer some strategies that are fairly easy to implement and have strong potential for creating a climate for action and change. You'll think of others as your advocacy involvement grows, but consider some of these ideas to help you get started:

Level 1—Ten Minutes or Less

- **Write postcards.** Enlist persons in your congregation or social network to write postcards to their legislators about one specific issue. Write out a sample text for them to personalize. Provide the stamps if you can.
- **Make a phone call.** Write out three or four sentences, practice your "speech," and call your legislator's office. Ask to speak with the legislator, but be prepared to give your message to staff.
- **Send an e-mail message.** Go to the website of a major advocacy organization (see appendix B) and use their technology to send a message to your public officials.
- **Learn the names and addresses of your elected representatives and senators.** Again, websites of advocacy organizations usually have tools that will give you that information based on your home address.

Level 2—Thirty Minutes or More

- **Register to vote.** Ask your church to designate a voter registration month and pray for this endeavor. Encourage often-not-registered people to go with you: older teens, new residents in your neighborhood, parents of young children.
- **Vote.** Mount a get-out-the-vote initiative in your church with posters and reminders. Offer older persons and parents of young children a ride to the polls.
- **Compose a fact sheet.** Gather some pertinent facts and figures about a critical child and family issue. Put

the information into flyers, and share them with your friends, neighbors, and people at your church.

Level 3—Two Hours or More

- **Attend a community forum.** Listen to the perspectives of others in your community and ask questions of the elected officials in attendance. Make a short presentation about your position on the issue being discussed.
- **Join a coalition.** Work with others already engaged in organizing an advocacy and public-policy initiative. Determine whether you want to focus on local or statewide efforts.
- **Work in a political campaign.** Help a good candidate get elected by volunteering at her or his campaign office. Make phone calls, stuff envelopes, host a coffee gathering, or help organize a community rally.

The tools located in appendixes D, E, and F will help you initiate some of the advocacy strategies listed above.

Challenging Systems

As we consider ways to speak truth to power on behalf of those who have little power, we must take a close look at all the institutions and systems in our communities, indeed, in our daily lives. In the church we often focus on the issues and shortcomings of individuals (e.g., jealousy, impatience, anger), and ignore the systems of injustice (e.g., poverty, racism, lack of health care, inadequate school funding in poor neighborhoods) that shape our lives and perceptions. We must learn to ask: "How does this church (or neighborhood organization or city department or local school) affect the lives of children, youth, and their families? Does it contribute to their overall welfare and to the common good of the community? Or does it bring harm to their lives and futures?"

We look deeper, and we ask more questions, "What can we in the church do to make these institutions (or these systems or these communities) work more effectively with and for children?" "How can I/we work to build a community that exhibits love, mercy, and justice for all God's children?" "How do we build relationships with children, youth, and families who live in communities that are very different from our own?" These are not questions that have quick solutions, but Jesus calls us to explore these issues in light of our commitment to the gospel. Acting on those questions is a central aspect of our commitment as child advocates.

Comprehensive Approach

Advocacy forms the link between short-term and long-term planning, between direct service and systemic change, between individual acts of mercy and organized action for justice. Advocates often start with an individual situation and then make a larger commitment as they learn more about the issue.

Tutoring a child who speaks a language other than English could be an impetus to get involved in bilingual education. As you work with this one child, you realize that there are other children in her class that do not speak English fluently. You talk with the teacher, find a bilingual person to assist your efforts, and meet with the parents. As time goes on, you research the bilingual education standards, attend a school board meeting, write letters to the local newspaper, or contribute articles to the church newsletter. Listening carefully to the parents generates useful plans and strategies. They have good ideas about how the school could be more helpful to their children, and they can help to organize a small coalition of parents, teachers, and other advocates to work on increasing educational services for children with language differences.

For every individual or local need, there is a corresponding issue that encompasses a much larger group of people. Every problem that we attempt to address has a root cause. Christ calls us to respond to one child's individual pain or need. Christ also calls us to address the underlying causes of that pain and need. Tutoring one child with limited English skills is a worthy thing to do. Organizing a broad-based educational initiative for a group of children and parents not yet fluent in English is another important way to minister to community families. Acting on the public-policy issues related to children with limited English skills and their families—school funding, bilingual education, immigration reform—is equally important for the well-being of these children and families. Public policy matters!

The Power of Numbers

Recently, Laura Dean talked with a group of people who were not having a lot of success getting people in their churches involved in public-policy issues. Janelle told the group about her efforts to organize a meeting on immigration issues. She invited a well-known expert to address the group, did a lot of publicity, and encouraged friends and colleagues to come. To her dismay, only 11 people attended the meeting. Several in the group agreed with Janelle that small numbers discouraged them. Others suggested that a small number of people passionate about an important issue is a good place to start.

Nancy Amidei, Senior Lecturer at the University of Washington and Director of the Civic Engagement Project, agrees with the latter point of view. In her advocacy workshops, she often points out that small numbers of people have, in fact, had a great impact on advocacy and public-policy. For example, one grief-stricken mother founded Mothers' Against Drunk Driving (MADD)[9] and three persons launched the hospice movement.[10] A small group of women who could not afford to pay for their mammograms created the impetus that challenged and changed the Medicare rules.[11] Significant policy changes have emerged from the small beginnings of these advocacy efforts.

Typically, about 2,000 bills are introduced each year in state legislatures across the country. About 350 to 400 of these bills are passed into law. Studies show that about 20% of registered voters contact their legislators at some point during the year. When legislators are asked the question, "How many calls to your office does it take to get your attention," the answer is typically, "About 12, especially if they are registered voters."[12]

Church people are well accustomed to recruiting persons to serve on boards or committees, assist with Vacation Bible school, or attend a mission dinner. We already possess some good basic skills in organizing. Now, we need to transfer that skill to the important work of convincing 12, or maybe 15, people to call our legislators, school board members, or village trustees about legislation that affects children and families.

Thinking theologically about public policy issues is an urgent task for people of all faith traditions. Public officials and elected representatives need to hear our voices on behalf of vulnerable children, youth, and families. We have knowledge and experience that will help them do a better job of crafting legislation and developing budgets. Our church leaders and friends also need to hear our voices. We can help them think and act theologically when considering children and youth issues in the congregation, community, state, nation, or world.

The warp is in place on the loom, and now it is time to add the weft. Just as the warp and weft weave in and out to create a piece of fabric, the direct service and public policy dimensions of advocacy weave together to build a just community for children of all ages. Our advocacy on their behalf cannot be fully effective until we pay as much attention to systems (public policy) as we do to services (programs). Our mission is clear—to do justice, love kindness, and walk humbly with our God—and our commitment is strong. As people of faith, we remember that advocacy is a spiritual discipline that compels us to engage our churches in public policy issues on behalf of the least, the last and the lost.

Questions for Reflection

1. Which model—silent, vocal, spirited—is your church most like? Why do you suppose that is the case? Are you comfortable with your church's particular stance? Why or why not?

2. Consider the tools and strategies your church uses to resolve conflict. How well do these strategies serve the congregation when members debate controversial matters? What are some other strategies or resources that might help members of the church work on sensitive issues in a less conflictual style?

3. Think about the social justice ministries that your church offers to the community (e.g., child care, tutoring, citizenship classes). What are the root causes of the issues that bring children and families to your outreach programs?

What can you do to help church members understand these issues more fully?

Action Steps

1. Do some research and determine some of the public policy initiatives that address those root causes. Share your newfound insight with others in the congregation.
2. Find out the names and addresses of your congressional or state legislators. Take the first step (or more!) toward developing a relationship with at least one of the public officials (e.g., write a letter, attend a community forum, visit her or him in the district office). Report the results of your visit to the Church Council or the Social Action Committee.
3. Identify one public policy issue for which you have knowledge or passion and do one thing to address that issue (e.g., join a coalition, write a letter to the editor of your local newspaper, lead a study group). Refer to the list of strategies on pp. 138–139 to get more ideas.

Chapter 8 Notes

1. For a broader discussion of Wesley's commitment to the poor, see the Task Force for the Bishops' Initiative on Children and Poverty, *Theological and Biblical Foundations: The Episcopal Initiative on Children and Poverty,* (Nashville: Cokesbury, 1997). Another useful resource on this topic is *Community with Children and the Poor: A Congregational Guide,* (Nashville: Cokesbury, 2003), 11–12.
2. Contact Protestants for the Common Good, 77 West Washington Street, #1124, Chicago, IL 60602, 312-223-9544, www.thecommongood.org for more information about the relationship between faith and politics through its education events and bi-weekly, electronic newsletter on social justice issues.
3. Protestants for the Common Good, *The Spirited Church in the Public World: A Handbook for Christian Political Activism,* (Chicago: Protestants for the Common Good, 2000), 13–15.
4. Ibid., 15–23.
5. Ibid., 23–26

6. See pages 8–11 of *The Spirited Church in the Public World* for a broader discussion of church and state issues.

7. See Paul Chaffee's book, *Accountable Leadership: A Resource Guide for Sustaining Legal, Financial, and Ethical Integrity in Today's Congregations* (San Francisco: Jossey-Bass, 1997) for more information on tax issues and churches.

8. Contact JUSTPEACE, Center for Mediation and Conflict Transformation, 100 Maryland Ave. NE, Washington, D.C. 20002, 202-488-5647, www.JUSTPEACE umc.org. Another good resource is the Lombard Mennonite Peace Center, 630-627-0507, www.LMPeaceCenter.org.

9. Go to www.alcohol.bitglyph.com to read a condensed version of Candy Lightner's story of her daughter's death and the founding of MADD.

10. Go to www.nhpco.org, the website for the National Hospice and Palliative Care Organization, to learn about the contributions of Dame Cicely Saunders, Florence Walk, and Elisabeth Kubler-Ross.

11. Nancy Amidei shared these examples of the power of individuals, singly or in small groups, in the workshop, "Your Vote Counts," at the Quadrennial Conference for Community Ministries and Institutions, General Board of Global Ministries in Houston, November 13, 1999.

12. Ibid.

CHAPTER 9

Taking Risks for Children

⟨ Discipleship and Stewardship ⟩

Story

At work in her local church, Diane was assisting with serving communion. Children had only recently been invited to participate in communion in that church, and she wondered in the first few services if the children had any understanding of what was happening. It was obvious from their expressions and joy as they approached the table that they anticipated taking communion, but what could they know about its meaning? At this service, two sisters knelt at the communion rail with their dad, and looked intently at Diane as she approached with the bread. Often, when very young children are receiving communion she diverts from the commonly used words, "This is the body of Christ," using instead, "This is because God loves you." She said those words to the sisters, who responded, "We know!" clearly and with enthusiasm.

Later, Diane wondered, how do these young girls know that God loves them? Who has taught them that absolute trust in God? Who has taken the steps necessary to allow these children to experience and know God's love at the ages of four and five? The answer must be a variety of people who took action on their behalf to ensure they knew and trusted God from the very beginning of their lives: parents, grandparents, other family members, nursery workers, Sunday school teachers, friends, and individuals in the congregation. Teaching or sharing faith with children, and including them in the community are forms of child advocacy. As persons who care for children and as people of faith, advocacy becomes stewardship and discipleship.

Scripture

All three of the synoptic Gospels (Matthew, Mark, Luke) tell the story of Jesus healing an epileptic boy at the request of the boy's father. In Mark 9:14–27, the story begins with Jesus noticing a commotion in a crowd around some of his disciples. There was a father there who said his son had a demon, and the disciples were unable to cast it out. The father asked Jesus to cast out the demon if he was able. Jesus became a little perturbed with the "if you are able" phrase, and said, "Don't you believe I can do this?" The father said, "Yes, I believe. Help my unbelief!" At that, Jesus cast the demon from the boy, and the boy was healed. So exhausted was the boy that the spectators thought he was dead. "But Jesus took him by the hand and lifted him up, and he was able to stand."[1] The same story is told in Matthew, with the ending "For truly I tell you, if you have faith the size of a mustard seed, you will say to this mountain, Move from here to there, and nothing will be impossible for you".[2] At this point Jesus, according to Luke, takes the boy back to his father, and those watching were astounded at the greatness of God.

In this Scripture, we see the father taking a risk for the boy, going first through the crowds, who must have looked down upon this child as possessed, as possibly evil, certainly as different. Then he went to the disciples, who tried to cast out the demon but were unable. There is no indication of how long they tried, but we do know that a crowd gathered around this spectacle. The father, not to be dissuaded by the failure of the power and authority of the disciples turned to Jesus, and said, "Teacher, I brought you my child. Heal him if you are able." Jesus is upset with the lack of faith of both the father and the disciples. Then Jesus assumes an advocacy role as he heals, and again as he gives the child back to the father.

Making a difference for children is difficult to do. There are times when it feels like all of society works against child advocates; money is inaccessible, resources are unavailable, and positive changes seem to be only distant dreams. Further, there are often risks in advocacy, in stepping out in an often countercultural way to take action for children. These risks include: effects of alternative use of resources; being viewed by one's peers, staff, or society in general as single-minded or different; questioning authority with possible repercussions; and sometimes facing failure. It isn't always easy. It is often risky. It is an expression of faith. Child advocacy is an expression of one's faith through discipleship and through stewardship.

Discipleship Defined

Discipleship is an interesting and multifaceted word. In John 13:34–35, Jesus tells the disciples that if they show love for one another (as Jesus loved them) everyone will know they are disciples of Jesus. Advocacy defined as taking action on behalf of children is action that will make the lives of children fuller and healthier, and is certainly showing love for them. In Luke 14, discipleship is defined again as carrying the cross and following Jesus. In taking action for children, we are often carrying a cross as we confront authority and power and demand justice for children. We are often burdened by systems that place children last and policies that relegate their needs to the back of the financial bus.

Another definition of discipleship is to follow Jesus, which means to live according to the teachings and example of Jesus. For many years, bracelets, posters, and email signatures have proclaimed the question "What would Jesus do?" Discipleship means doing what Jesus would have done. Throughout this book there have been many illustrations of this kind of discipleship, from putting children first to making a difference in the life of one child through mentoring or child care or political action. Child advocacy is discipleship, and it will transform the world as it makes a difference for even one child.

Child advocacy is an expression of one's faith through discipleship and through stewardship.

A related definition of discipleship is learning from Jesus. A disciple is a learner, one who recognizes what is seen rather than sees what is already known. Diane, while working in a suburban church, saw this kind of learning firsthand. The children's ministries at that church were growing and, each year, claiming more space for learning and community building. The church was a product of an educational era where children sat in desks in rows in small spaces; hence, the classrooms were small and narrow. The congregation saw only that the space was inadequate, but it stayed with the outdated educational model because of the space restrictions. Diane saw, instead, an opportunity. She talked and listened to architects, engineers, and construction experts. Within two years, all non-weight bearing walls were taken down. The new space was carpeted and freshly painted, creating a marvelous space for the faith-building needs of the children and their families. Compare Diane's advocacy efforts to those of the father in the story above. She stepped out and made a difference for children as she enlisted the help of others in the church. She was persistent in her advocacy efforts, and learned how to provide the space needed for the children's learning and faith growth.

For this book, discipleship is also one of the weft threads. Woven into the warp threads, we begin to see our fabric of child advocacy. The weft threads of discipleship surround our warp threads of the realities of children's lives, the issues, and the methods to advocate for children. Discipleship ties our faith into the weaving, knowing that as advocates we follow Jesus as we make a difference for children.

Child Advocacy as Discipleship

Actually, *Child Advocacy as Discipleship* could have been the title of this book, because as disciples of Jesus Christ, it is our mandate to transform the world. As child advocates, the focus is on transforming the world for children. In a 2004 gathering of the Council of Bishops of The United Methodist Church, our United Methodists bishops again proclaimed the mission of the church to be disciple making for world transformation. They listed seven vision pathways toward this mission. Several relate to this book and the work and ministry of child advocates, but two are clearly and strongly related: reaching and transforming the lives of new generations of children and eliminating poverty in community with those who are poor.[3] Discussed previously by Bishops Dyck and Jung in the foreword, this reminds us here of the vital importance and timeliness of the expression of child advocacy as discipleship.

Discipleship involves constant learning and growth in faith. Being a disciple is being a pupil, one who is on a lifelong journey. Discerning a solution to a child's need and taking action toward that solution is one step of a journey, and much will be learned along the way. Further, like the example of the church building above, a solution for this day is not necessarily one that will last into the next decade or next generation or even next year, in some cases. Methods, theories, and systems all change over time, and require new solutions given new requirements. Years ago, a huge part of a child advocate's job was to find information to support efforts to address the needs of children. Today, given the instant access most advocates have to information via Internet and email, finding the information has become much faster. New challenges include how to sift through great quantities of information and how to determine reliability of data. Advocacy as discipleship is learning and growing in faith.

Stewardship Defined

Stewardship is the responsibility we have to maintain and use wisely the gifts God has given us. For the child advocate, stewardship is multifaceted. It is stewardship of resources, which requires a redistribution of precious resources to allow for the care of children who lack the basics of health care, education, food and water, safety, and access to these. It is stewardship of time, that advocates' precious time might be spent in the best possible ways. Likewise, it is in the stewardship of talent that advocates' efforts might make the greatest impact in making differences for children. In our advocacy weaving, the image around which this book is written, stewardship is one of the weft threads. It is one that ties the rest together. As we care for the children, we live our faith.

The Stewardship Role of Parents

As disciples, we are all called to advocate for children. But the story of the healing of the epileptic boy at the beginning of this chapter recognizes that the parent is the one who is ultimately best to care for a child for the long term. Jesus gives the child back to the father. This assumes, of course, a parent who is able to advocate and care for a child. We all know there are those among us who are not.

Karen Marie Yust[4] suggests that perhaps it's time for unofficial godparenting. These are godparents who practice intentional nurture and relationship with children, though they have no "official" ties to the child. These practices are consistent with the baptismal promises each adult makes at a child's baptism, and might include affirmation, recognition, and support. She says it is a way of communicating God's love through persons to children, and helps kids know what God's love is like.

We know that parents come in many varieties: biological (formerly called "natural"), adoptive, foster, grandparents, and many others, including Yust's "unofficial" godparents. We use the word *parent* to describe the fathering/mothering role of a person who has primary responsibility for a child, whether the biological parent or any other person who steps into this role. In a sense, parenting is the stewardship action of those who have taken on the role of father/mother to a child; they are stewards of that child's growth and well-being as the child matures into adulthood.

The Stewardship Role of Congregations

At the same time, we see many people taking a part in the advocacy for the boy in the healing story we examined above—the disciples, Jesus, and the father, who recognized that he could not do it by himself. In this story we encounter the importance of the many systems in place in the church and the world to assist parents as they raise their children to be healthy and whole adults.

A congregation actively supports and nurtures families in many ways. They provide a safe and sacred place to experience God and resources to families on ways to take this into the home. They welcome children in worship, and teach them to worship God in many ways. Churches prepare children to affirm and claim their faith, usually in adolescence in confirmation or similar processes. They celebrate milestones along life's journey with faith-related markers: the first Bible, the "graduation" to various levels of classes, the completion of a variety of steps in Christian growth.

Baptismal Vows

Much of the stewardship and discipleship work of both the congregation and parents as stewards of children is mandated by fulfilling baptismal vows. In The United Methodist Church, parents or sponsors are asked to reaffirm their faith and then are specifically asked if they will "nurture these children in Christ's holy Church, that by your teaching and example they may be guided to accept God's grace for themselves" and to "lead a Christian life"—to be disciples.[5] The congregation is then asked to avow that they will nurture not only one another but these new persons through their care, their love, and their forgiveness. And again after the actual laying on of hands—the baptism—the members of the congregation affirm their statements and repeat their promises of membership in the body of Christ. These are promises of stewardship: the people promise to faithfully participate in the church by the sharing of their prayers, presence, gifts, and service. They pledge to take care of this new member, one another, and the church.

This is a big commitment, and given the state of children in our country and in the world today, we wonder how many of us think about these promises as we participate in the baptism of children in our churches. Child advocacy is an inevitable result of the baptismal vows, as these vows are lived by the family and the congregation.

Doing Our Best

There is a recent book available via download called *Homeland Insecurity: American Children at Risk* at www.everychildmatters.org/homelandinsecurity/HomelandInsecurityBooklet.pdf. "We can do so much better" are words that can summarize every page of that report. For example, while we have made great strides in health coverage, for example, for children, with the Comprehensive Health Insurance Programs of various states, we can do so much better. There are still miles to go in alleviating child abuse and neglect; we can do so much better. National child abuse statistics are gruesome,[6] yet seem to be showing slight improvement. But the question is still how many cases of child abuse are too many, and for child advocates the answer is "one." Head Start and other early childhood programs are underfunded, yet studies show over and over again how much can be saved in terms of quality of children's lives and in actual funding dollars if early childhood issues are addressed. *We can do so much better.* This book details many painful statistics regarding our children and the ways we treat them, but it also shows that we do have solutions for the problems of our children. We simply haven't made them—our children and the children of the world—our priority.

The Children's Defense Fund[7] started a program called the Child Watch Visitation Program, which is a good example of how advocates can move children's issues up the priority ladder with public officials and leaders of church, school, business, and others. In this program, executives and politicians, clergy and business leaders, are taken to the real world of children and families. They visit schools and community ministries and church-based child care centers. They show how the issues children are facing today can be alleviated by changes in systems, by revisions in funding, and by additional participation of the community. They highlight both problems and solutions, teaching the community leaders that there is hope. Leaders leave the Child Watch Visitation Program inspired to make a difference for children. They become child advocates, taking action for children.

Advocacy is, again, a matter of stewardship and discipleship. It is stewardship of our resources—shall we use them to help children or to increase the defense budget? Shall we build a bigger office for the photocopier or install safety windows in the nursery?

And it is also discipleship: What would Jesus do? How do we follow Jesus in this and other issues relating to children? What can we learn from the current issues regarding children and how do we grow in faith as we address them? Where does Scripture relate to these issues? Where do we see Jesus leading us through them? How can each one of us, child advocates, make a difference, and take an action to better the lives of a child? As we write, we are reminded of the traditional song of the drummer boy at the birth of the incarnated God in Bethlehem. What can we give? What gifts do we have to share to make a difference in the lives of children?

Questions for Reflection

1. Read Mark 9:14–27 in your study Bible, and compare it to Matthew 17:14–21 and Luke 9:37–43a. What do the three versions of this story have in common, and what makes them different?

2. Think about the relationship between your child advocacy and discipleship. How is the action you take on behalf of children faithful and world transforming? What does your faith tell you about children that compels you to take action on their behalf?

3. Have you ever considered your responsibility toward children as an issue of stewardship? How do you use your resources to care for children of your church and of the world?

4. Recall a time when your actions have made a difference for a child or for a group of children, a time when you have clearly been a child advocate. Has this action had an effect on your faith life? Consider ways you "grew in faith" as a result of this advocacy?

Action Steps

1. Look at the baptismal service for your denomination. Look at how your church is fulfilling these vows for children who are baptized in your community. Is there something you can do to add to existing ministries?

2. Check into the Child Watch Visitation Program or other similar programs in your community. Can you get your church involved in this, or do something similar in your church or community?

3. List your own gifts in child advocacy, and think about using them in new ways with community groups or with parents or other caregivers this week to make a difference for a child.

Chapter 9 Notes

1. Mark 9:27.
2. Matthew 17:19.
3. "Bishops Act on Episcopal Address, Global Concerns," United Methodist News Service release #627, November 8, 2005.
4. Karen Marie Yust, *Real Kids, Read Faith, Practices for Nurturing Children's Spiritual Lives*, (San Francisco: Jossey-Bass, 2004).
5. *The United Methodist Hymnal* (Nashville: The United Methodist Publishing House, 1989), 34.
6. For statistical information on child abuse, see www.preventchildabuse.org, the web site of Prevent Child Abuse America. They also have good information on current legislation and methods for advocacy.
7. Children's Defense Fund, 25 E. Street NW, Washington, DC 20001, www.childrensdefense.org.

CHAPTER 10

Weaving a Future for All Children

Vocation as Advocacy

Story

Diane dished out canned peaches in a serving line at a church-based feeding program. The basement of the church was rather dingy, in spite of the good efforts of a number of helping people. The floor tiles were faded and worn. The functional folding chairs needed a good scrubbing and the tables were chipped and scratched. There were no amenities. No color brightened the room. The trays were the same dingy gray as the tables and floor. The food was predictable: hot dogs, beans, canned fruit, cookies, and a scoop of macaroni salad. People started coming through the line at 5:00, and kept coming as the line closed at 6:30. "When can we have seconds?" was the most often asked question, followed by, "Any milk left over to take home?"

Soup kitchens, dignity diners, open kitchens, open tables, whatever they are called, operate to serve food to the hungry. This scene is repeated all over the country that night and every night, but on this particular night, Diane was surprised by the number of children in the group. Single parents, grandparents, babysitters, and two parents brought their children to the church for food and with the hope of some milk to take home. A hungry boy's eyes grew large as he eyed his tray with anticipation. Other children sat in their little groups laughing and trading their food. One boy traded his cookies for his brother's hot dog, but realizing his brother's remaining food wouldn't be enough for him, soon gave him back a portion of the hot dog. Spanish and English mixed in their conversations. A little girl picked up her crying younger sister and comforted her. God was there, in the love, in the conversation, in the laughter, and in the opportunity provided by having enough to eat that day. But the question stood like the proverbial elephant in the room: "Why are there hungry children in this wealthy land? What can be done to change the system that disables working families with hunger and want?"

Scripture

At that very hour some Pharisees came and said to him, "Get away from here, for Herod wants to kill you." He said to them, "Go and tell that fox for me 'Listen, I am casting out demons and performing cures today and tomorrow, and on the third day I finish my work. Yet today, tomorrow and the next day I must be on my way, because it is impossible for a prophet to be killed outside of Jerusalem.' Jerusalem, Jerusalem the city that kills the prophets and stones those who are sent to it! How often have I desired to gather your children together as a hen gathers her brood under her wings, and you were not willing. See, your house is left to you. And I tell you, you will not see me until the time comes when you say, 'Blessed is the one who comes in the name of the Lord.'" (Luke 13:31–35)

In this brief section of Luke, Jesus restates his ministry to heal and to live out his calling, unstopped by fear of those in power. He also suggests his unseen presence working in others in his name, that Christ working in us may be recognized in the service we do and in the world we change for even one child. We, child advocates, are called to heal, unstopped by fear of those in power. We work in the name of Jesus Christ, who dwells in us. And as advocates, we lament over Jerusalem (or Chicago, Minneapolis-St. Paul, Dayton, Bonita Springs, or Las Vegas) when our eyes are opened, and we see the depth and breadth of the needs of the children. We lament over the hunger of the children in the soup kitchen and those on the street, and we resolve to find ways to make a difference.

Throughout this book we have been weaving a fabric of advocacy. We began with the essentials of the loom: a theological foundation, biblical and historical imperatives for advocacy, and an understanding of the world of children today. We dressed the loom with the warp (vertical) threads: the practices, issues, and tools of child advocates in chapters 4 through 7. Then we began to weave our fabric with the weft threads of acting for change in public policy, discipleship, and stewardship, and now, in this chapter, vocation. One of Diane's seminary professors[1] defined vocation as the intersection of a person's gifts and the needs of the world. We have articulated the needs of the children in many places, and we now call you to the task of determining where your gifts intersect those needs. We believe that God calls all of us to find that intersection. In this chapter, we examine three ways through which you might discern the intersection of your gifts and the needs of the world: *dream, pray* and *work*.[2]

Dream

As Christians and as child advocates, we dream. Our dreams include the elimination of poverty, and the health and well-being of every child, including enough to eat every day, a safe place to live, a worthy education, a good place to play, and someone to give love as well as receive love from children. We have attempted to point out that while all children face some challenges and difficulties in their lives, the challenges and difficulties affecting some children are exacerbated by poverty. The fact that they are poor means that they are ill more often, hungry many days, less likely to do well in school, and more likely to die before their first birthdays.

Our dream, therefore, is the hope that we, as servants of Jesus Christ, will contribute in our little and big ways to the beloved community, the reign of God that refuses to accept the suffering of children. We dream that we will be part of the beloved community that ensures that all children are valued and that all children understand themselves to be a valued part of that community. In a plenary session at Focus 2005, Dr. Fred Smith[3] declared that the beloved community is a movement, not a static moment in time. It is the empowerment of God in the world to make a difference for children and the poor, but also to us as we create a world that is ruled by justice, peace, and love. Everyone in the beloved community is valued, loved unconditionally, and participates in shalom, that wholeness in love requiring action on behalf of others—advocacy.

> *Loving children is at the heart of this book; loving children through faithful witness and practice of advocacy makes a difference in their lives.*

We live in the midst of the beloved community even as we long for—dream—of its coming. We see glimpses of it in our own children's faces, in the eagerness of children at the altar for communion, in the eyes of a newborn at a family shelter, in the comforting embrace of sisters in a soup kitchen. We experience the beloved community as we develop relationships of mutuality and friendship with children, youth, and families who live beyond our comfortable communities and churches. Every time we dish up peaches, every time we work to prevent child abuse, every time we listen to the stories of children, every time we speak up to our legislators, we participate in the beloved community. Every time we let children know they are loved, valued, important, and gifted, we open the beloved community to children. And we bring the beloved community closer each time we take action for children, particularly those who live in poverty or life-threatening distress. The beloved community is here and is coming in our hopes and our dreams of a better world for children.[4]

One place both of us have felt the powerful presence of the beloved community is at the Proctor Institute for Child Advocacy Ministry,[5] sponsored every summer by the Children's Defense Fund. With equal parts of family reunion, spiritual renewal, and skill building, the gathering is an inspiring week of sermons, workshops, and reflection groups focused on the needs of children and celebrating our calls to advocacy. Held at the lovely Alex Haley Farm in Clinton, Tennessee, the Institute provides a hospitable learning environment in an atmosphere of inclusion and celebration of diversity. The Proctor Institute is a place where we can articulate our dreams for children and be "fed" intellectually and spiritually so that we continue our advocacy journeys with joy and conviction.

In our United Methodist Church, we are led by a Council of Bishops, which sets forth the vision of our mission to make disciples and thereby transform the world. Our bishops have articulated seven vision pathways,[6] two of which relate directly to advocating for children: "reaching and transforming the lives of the new generations of children" and "eliminating poverty in community with the poor."[7] The vision pathways express our bishops' dream of advocating for children. A "unity" resolution adopted by the Council of Bishops and the United Methodist general agencies prior to the 2008 General Conference reaffirms this dream through a new agenda emphasizing "ministry with the poor, particularly children."[8]

Other denominations have their own versions of these pathways, resolutions, and visions. The Presbyterian Church wrote its "A Vision for Children and the Church" in 1993, and the Episcopal Church's "A Children's Charter for the Church, 1997" was supplemented in 2003 with a "Receiving the Child" Study Guide. In addition, the National Council of Churches produced "Church and Children: Vision and Goals for the 21st Century" in December 2004. See your denominational web-sites[9] for this and additional information.

Each of us in the local church takes the direction given by the denomination's leadership, the spiritual renewal and skill-building education of experiences like the Proctor Institute for Child Advocacy, the dreams of theologians like Fred Smith, and our own dreams, and weaves them into our advocacy fabric. We must see advocacy as an integral part of our ministries—of all our ministries, including worship, service, education, and nurture. Bishop Leontine T. C. Kelly wrote a commentary in which we believe she summed up the vocational call of the child advocate. She said, "I must love children. I must love children enough to teach them the causes of the problems of the world as well as I can analyze them, and never permit them to feel that they are superior to any other child. My love and caring for them must be so deep and so assuring that it will distill the pervasive fear of . . . war, the inevitability of hunger, starvation, poverty, and oppression. I must love children into believing they are the hope of the world." [10]

Loving children is at the heart of this book; loving children through faithful witness and practice of advocacy makes a difference in their lives. We weave these dreams into our fabric as the threads of the weft, those that help hold the finished product together and give it substance, strength, and beauty.

Pray

As disciples of Jesus Christ and as child advocates, we pray. Every time we hear the news or read the paper, we are newly aware of the hurt so many children endure, the overwhelming odds they must overcome each day, and the small triumphs of individual children and families. The individual prayers of each advocate are vitally important to making a difference in the lives of children. Praying, an essential element of our discipleship, links our faith directly to advocacy. As advocates, we must commit to a daily prayer life that reaches beyond our own concerns to those of the children in the wider community and across the world. We must pray often and earnestly for God's *kindom*[11] of justice and peace to be realized.

In addition to individual, constant prayer for children, our work as advocates is strengthened and supported by corporate prayer; that is, the shared prayer of our faith community. This community may be the local church, annual conference, or all advocates gathered at an event such as Focus.[12] Diane's local church, Fridley United Methodist Church, has several prayer groups through which we pray for children, including the UMW circles, Sunday school classes, a prayer chain, and a weekly hour of prayer. We pray for God's abiding presence with us and with the children, for specific concerns of children in trouble—children in our local churches, in the wider community, and all around the world.

When we think about our vocations—those places in which our gifts meet the needs of the world—we recognize that one of the gifts we bring to that intersection is the power of prayer. Further, we know that many of the greatest needs of the world are those of the children. We have outlined some of the critical issues that confront and confound children and their families. Our prayers cry out for the alleviation of those ills and injustices, even as we request strength and wisdom for ourselves and others as we urge those in power to be just and as we work toward justice. We must pray for one another "without ceasing," that we might have the courage to effect change individually and together. This is our vocation as Christians, as child advocates. The vocation of advocacy is a call to pray, to ask for God's presence in us and through us to change the world for children.

Along with many other houses of worship across the country, Diane's church observes Children's Sabbath on the third weekend of every October. Refer to chapter 5 for an explanation of the observance of Children's Sabbath. After the sermon on one Children's Sabbath Sunday, she asked worshipers of all ages to write down one thing they would do for children. Answers included recognizing children, working at a neighborhood clothes closet, hugging a grandchild, reading books to the kids in the child care center, praying for children, and spending time with a little brother. At the next year's Children's Sabbath, Diane posted these answers on a bulletin. During worship, she reminded people of their promises, and asked if they had carried out their commitments. More important, she reminded them that even their small efforts on behalf of a child or a group of children can bring hope and healing.

Work

As people of faith and as child advocates, we work. The biblical examples of child advocates discussed in chapter 2 suggested that advocates were strong, brave, persistent, collaborative, and assertive. These characteristics are like muscles that move the body as it works in advocacy. Laura Dean remembers an image offered by Dr. Antonia Darder[13]in an antiracism workshop for early childhood professionals. Dr. Darder said, "Courage is like a muscle. The more you work it, the stronger it gets." She pointed out that muscles are effective only when they are exercised so that they become stronger and stronger over time. We encounter substantial barriers in our advocacy endeavors, but our courage grows stronger every time we take a risk, confront an injustice, or suggest a new way of thinking or doing. So it is with persistence, assertiveness, and all of the other attributes of the child advocate. It takes work—hard work—to strengthen and sustain those abilities.

Often we face feelings of helplessness. The issues that affect the lives of children are legion, and the solutions do not emerge easily. As people of faith, we often find ourselves overwhelmed, and we sometimes doubt that we can make a difference. We want to believe that we can bring positive change for children. We believe the words of Jesus, "All things can be done for the one who believes,"[14] but still we cry with the father of the epileptic boy, "I believe. Help my unbelief."[15]

At times like these, we must recognize and claim our power. Church people do have power, individually and corporately. We can influence what happens with children in the congregation, neighborhood, and the global community. We have a say in what takes place in the state legislature, city council, or village board. In fact, each member of the congregation has a civic responsibility—fueled by our understanding of discipleship—to communicate with our church leaders, our community organizations, and our elected representatives, including the governor and the president, about those issues for which we have knowledge or concern.

We must think of ourselves as experts. We are! We know things about our children, families, and communities that our church leaders and elected representatives probably do not know. They need to hear from us. In addition, our community leaders and elected officials need to hear the perspectives of people of faith on the full range of community and public policy issues that affect the lives of children, youth, and other vulnerable groups.

Like most things in our world, it's about relationships. The persons you approach—whether pastor, bishop, school principal, mayor, senator, representative, or governor—may not always be responsive when you try to share your point of view. Persistence is important, but take it a step at a time. Make a phone call, send an e-mail message, or write a letter as a first effort. Sometimes you'll get a response in return; sometimes you will not. Attend congregational or community meetings being sponsored by the district superintendent or legislator. Stand in line, shake hands, introduce yourself and say, "I wrote to you about increasing education funding (or camp scholarships for children in low-income communities). I'm very concerned about this issue. Is there someone on your staff with whom I may speak?" Then, follow up with another letter or send a fact sheet on which you have written a personal note. Volunteer to be on an anti-gambling task force or a committee working on immigration reform.

You can also call the legislator's (or bishop's) office and make an appointment to meet with him/her or a staff person. Enlist someone to go with you, preferably another voter (or church member) who also lives in the legislator's district. It takes time, but gradually the legislator (conference leader) will come to recognize you, and will remember that you are knowledgeable on school funding, gambling, or immigration issues. One day you may get a call with a person saying, "Ms. Smith, we are organizing a focus group on education funding reform and would like to invite you to participate."

Recall for a moment the story of the saving of Baby Moses' life.[16] In this biblical story, ordinary women took extraordinary steps to respond to the unthinkable: a national policy of genocide for Hebrew boys. The actions of these women wove together—each woman's action made the next action possible—and became an essential part of God's plan to liberate the Hebrews from Egypt. They had not organized a committee on how to save Hebrew children—how could they? Instead, they collaborated: each woman, in her own way, did what she could to save this one child.

They dreamed, prayed, and worked by resisting evil, making quick decisions, cooperating across racial/cultural/religious/economic boundaries and taking extraordinary risks—and they changed the course of history.

Models of Advocacy Vocation

This is the vocation of child advocacy—being called out of our daily tasks and routines—to take ordinary and extraordinary actions with and on behalf of children and youth.

As we wrote this book, we learned about many other persons who claim child advocacy as their vocations. These people are of varied ages and economic situations. They live in all parts of the world. Some are famous, most are not. Some are no longer with us, but all remain as models for our advocacy ministries. They live and act at the intersection at which their gifts meet the needs of the children of the world.

We want you, our readers, to meet some of these ordinary/extraordinary child advocates:

- **Dr. Laurinda Quipungo**, the wife of a bishop in East Angola, serves as the health coordinator for the East Angola Conference. She also runs a clinic and personally cares for 24 orphans at the orphanage.
- **Rev. Sandra Olewine**, an American United Methodist pastor, serves in Bethlehem, ministering to a congregation who are like prisoners, unable to leave the city. The children, she says, have never seen anything outside of Bethlehem. Her ministry is to help them find hope.
- **Guy Hayes**, a leader of the West Africa Trauma Team, teaches skills in trauma counseling and healing in Liberia and Sierra Leone. His ministry, while not directly with children, changes the lives of children through the adults he teaches.
- **Cathy Skogen-Soldner**,[17] a gifted musician and writer, creates musicals and songs for children. Her lyrics echo the words of a prophet, urging us to feed, shelter, respect, and hold our children.

- **Mattie Stephanek,** a boy with a rare form of muscular dystrophy, died at age 13. He was an avid writer who said he believed God's language was the language of children. His hope was to share his thoughts and gifts with others to inspire them to help others. Through personal pain and suffering, he showed us that children are leaders and advocates for other children.[18]
- **You** can be a child advocate no matter what your age or economic situation or profession or gifts. Whether you are an ordinary person or an extraordinary person or, more likely, a combination of both, you can be a child advocate who can make a difference in the world for children.

The work of the child advocate is to take action on behalf of children. Throughout this book, we have listed biblical and historical imperatives for this action, critical issues on which we need to act, and methods for action in our local churches and in the world. As advocates, we hear God calling us to work for change, to make the world a better place for children. As advocates, we know how badly change is needed, and it is our task to act in a variety of ways to effect change. We draw courage from the women of Exodus, stand in solidarity with the father of the epileptic boy, and find our voice through the Canaanite women. We are prophets, often speaking truth to power in ways that make people uncomfortable, even angry. Prophets interpret God's will. They lift the need to change and disrupt the status quo. A plaque Diane has on her desk reminds her, "Prophets aren't called to be successful. They are called to be faithful."[19]

Our weaving in this book is finished, but the fabric we have created will never come off the loom—the loom's contributions are still essential, because there is much work to be done. We know that our children are living in poverty. They are hungry, and they are in need of medical care. They attend inadequate schools, and they need a just legal system. They are homeless, and they are forced to work too soon. They live in refugee camps, and they survive on the streets as prostitutes. Our response to the needs of children is to call the world to justice for all children. It is our vocation. It is our discipleship. It is our life's work and our greatest calling.

The LORD is my light and my salvation;
Whom shall I fear?
The LORD is the stronghold of my life;
Of whom shall I be afraid?
I believe that I shall see the
Goodness of the Lord
In the land of the living,
Wait for the LORD;
Be strong, and let your heart
Take courage.
Wait for the LORD! (Psalm 27: 1, 13–14)

Questions for Reflection

Dream

1. Describe the kindom of God for children, and recall
    Bishop Dyck's description of the button she wore that said
    "So! How are the children?" (See p. 11.) How does the
    idea of *kindom* relate to the Bishop's button?
2. Why do we title this section "Dream"?
3. Make a list of your dreams for children and youth. Reflect
    on how many of your dreams are about survival issues and
    how many relate to enrichment of their lives. Think about
    how your context (economic status, occupation, lifestyle)
    shapes your dreams for children. How might your dreams
    be different from a parent or pastor who lives in a com-
    munity characterized by poverty and distress?

Pray

1. In 1 Thessalonians 5:17, the apostle Paul said, "Pray with-
    out ceasing." What does that mean in the context of child
    advocacy? How does one pray without ceasing?
2. Make a commitment now to pray for children, and include
    children at every possibility in your own prayers and in
    the corporate prayers you offer. Think of the prayer groups
    at your own church and ways you can help others include
    children in the ongoing prayer life of these groups.

Work

1. Define prophet. Identify times in which you have been prophetic. What happened? How did your friends and family respond to you? What did members of your church think of your prophetic call to justice or mercy?
2. What makes people uncomfortable with change? What are some ways one can "speak truth to power"? How can people be helped to listen even out of discomfort?

Action Steps

Dream

1. Organize a public witness for children—a prayer vigil, a silent march, a concert in a park near the heart of your community. Proclaim a vision of health and wholeness for children and enlist participants in taking action on behalf of children in crisis in the community.
2. Plan a response to this book for your congregation or annual conference committee or an additional group with whom you work. Ask the group, "So, how are the children?" and discuss their responses with them. Help others catch the dream of making this world a better place for children.

Pray

1. Create a prayer calendar for children and adults to use throughout Advent or Lent to guide their prayers for children, youth, and families of all kinds and in all places. Be sure to include prayers for children who are hungry and those who have too much to eat, for children living in refugee camps and those who have two houses, for children with good health care and those with no health insurance.
2. Write prayers regarding child advocacy for use in your worship services, or submit prayer requests asking the congregation to pray for children.

Work

1. Think of other people who have worked as child advocates, who have been models of advocacy for you. Tell their stories to your congregation or your work groups. Invite known advocates in your area to visit your church to share their stories.

2. Invite your bishop, district superintendent, or lay leader (or other church leaders) to write a column or preach about his or her child advocacy and its importance as a part of ministry.

Chapter 10 Notes

1. From lecture notes on the work of Frederick Buechner, Dr. Rosemary Keller, Garrett Evangelical Theological Seminary.
2. Dream, pray, and work as a modality for the reign of God that has come and is coming was articulated in *Our Shared Dream: The Beloved Community* adopted and published by the Council of Bishops of the United Methodist Church, 2004.
3. Linda Green, "Building Community with Children," United Methodist News Service, August 8, 2005.
4. See The Council of Bishops of the United Methodist Church, *Our Shared Dream: The Beloved Community* (Nashville: Cokesbury, 2004) for an in-depth discussion of the Beloved Community.
5. Children's Defense Fund, www.childrensdefense.org or www.haleyfarm.org
6. See www.umc.org, Council of Bishops, for further information.
7. Tim Tanton, "Report on the October 30–November 4 meeting of the Council of Bishops of the United Methodist Church," United Methodist News Service, November 8, 2005.
8. The four mission initiatives are: leadership development; building new congregations and revitalizing existing ones; ministry with the poor (particularly children); combating the preventable diseases cultivated by poverty, such as malaria, HIV/AIDS, and tuberculosis. Detailed in an article in the *United Methodist Reporter* of the Northern Illinois Conference, June 8, 2007, by Marta Aldrich, Linda Green, and Fran Coode Walsh, UM Communications, Nashville.
9. www.pcusa.org, www.episcopalchurch.org, www.ncc.org.
10. Leontine T. C. Kelly, "I Must Love", *New World Outlook*, January 1985, 31.
11. Diane C. Olson, author of *Out of the Basement: A Holistic Approach to Children Ministries*, (Nashville: Disciplship Resources, 2001) explains this term to describe

the reign of God as a non-hierarchical, family-like community of humanity and God.

12. Focus is a national conference of persons in ministry with children, sponsored by the General Board of Discipleship every four years, usually in Nashville. Look for news of Focus at www.gbod.org.

13. Professor in Educational Policy Studies at the College of Education, University of Illinois at Champaign/Urbana, quoted from an anti-racism workshop at the annual conference of the National Association for the Education of Young Children in Atlanta, GA in November 1988.

14. Mark 9:23b

15. Mark 9:24b

16. See Exodus 2:1–10

17. Cathy's website is www.cathysmusic.com.

18. From Mattie's autobiographical entry at www.myhero.com.

19. There is no information on the plaque to give credit for this quote.

Study Guide

Study Guide

WE BELIEVE THAT group study is one way we can help people make meaning of their lives in the light of the Christian faith. Meaning created from this book will help persons live their discipleship in new ways and in ways that will change the lives of children. Our hope is that this study guide will be a map for group study of the book, but will be very flexible and easily used in a variety of settings.

- It may be used with a youth or adult group of any size. In groups over 12 persons, it is advisable to break into smaller groups for discussion. The basic format of this guide suggests three sessions, each one and a half hours long. It could, however, be used in six 45-minute to one-hour sessions (such as a Sunday school class) by focusing on the activities and discussions for one or two chapters at a session. Or the guide could be completed in a retreat setting, using all three sessions over a day and a half or two days. It could also be expanded beyond these time frames by including all of the learning options listed.
- In any setting, a leader might recommend study of the "Questions for Reflection" found at the end of each chapter at home between or before sessions. Members might

be asked to complete one of the "Action Steps" at the end of chapters studied during a session, and report back to the group at the next meeting. Another possibility is to do a group "Action Step" at the conclusion of the study of the book.

- In other words, we urge you to look at our study guide and individualize it to work best in your setting. You can use all of it or none—combine it with the questions and action steps at the ends of chapters or do something entirely separate from those. Consider the needs of the people of your group, the time you have to give to this study, and the results you wish to see as you determine how you will best use this guide.

Before Your Group Meets: Advance Preparation

A good leader is prepared to lead by prayer, study, and reflection.

Pray: Each time you work on the plans for a session, pray for the learners in your group and for knowledge of the Spirit's presence among you as you learn together.

Study: Read the chapters, review the questions, and gather supplemental information as well as necessary materials and equipment before the group meets.

Plan and Reflect: Think about how the group time will progress; plan the activities you will use to reinforce learning and create new learning. Evaluate your leadership as you go, and write down ideas for leadership the next time you meet or the next time you will lead this study.

It is always helpful to review group leadership process before you begin a study such as this. A good resource is the book titled *Leading Adult Learners* by Delia Halverson (Abingdon Press, 1995). Also helpful are sections on leadership in adult curriculum materials and at the General Board of Discipleship's website, www.gbod.org. Remembering that adults learn in many ways, we have provided options for reflection during the group sessions. You or your group may not be comfortable with all of them, but it is important to try to meet the needs of the learners in as many ways as possible. We urge you to be creative and play a bit with the options we list.

Several weeks before your group meets be sure all members have a copy of the book so they can read before the group meets. It is our experience that some group members will be better prepared than others with advance reading, but it will enhance discussion even if only one person has followed through. Before the first meeting, it would be helpful if persons have read at least the foreword, introduction, and chapter 1.

Creating and Building Community

A structure to your group meetings creates confidence in learners. They feel at ease knowing that there is a predictability or rhythm to the group meetings. Each time you meet, whether in an hour's session or one that will last a morning, we suggest you follow a basic format that flows from a gathering time through discussion and response, to reflection and closing.

The gathering time is very important in the formation of trust and inclusion in the group. Each time you meet, you may want to lead a welcoming or gathering ritual, and these are suggested in the lesson plans that follow for each session. While working on this book, Diane found it very helpful to create a small worship center near her computer. To the left of her desk is a bookcase, and on the top shelf, she placed a candle to remind her of the constant presence of the Spirit as she worked. Near the candle, she added various objects that reminded her of the reasons she was writing, and gave her strength and persistence when the writing became hard. There were five smooth stones, symbols of David's strength as he faced Goliath, a photo of her children, a card from a friend that said "Two girls in sneakers can do anything," and more. Around the shelf, on the wall, she taped newspaper articles, the writing schedule, and other written materials to help her focus and remember why we were writing this book.

You and your group may also want to create a worship center for your gathering time. A candle is a good way to help people remember

God's presence as you gather. It centers the gathering time in faith. You might provide a basic colored fabric cloth and candle, which you would use every time the group met, and add other objects as the group invests meaning in them. For example, in the section that includes chapter 5 regarding venues for advocacy, you may want to add a map of your city or area to the worship center, or a photo of your church or a child-serving agency near you. We've listed a few ideas in each session, but be creative and personal in your choices of objects in your worship center. Viewing these articles during group sessions will reinforce learning and link the group to the "real" world.

You may also wish to "build" a bulletin board or poster of current events relating to children and advocacy over the times you gather. Begin with a newspaper article or web printout of an example of children who need advocates, and encourage participants to bring in current event materials as they find them. It will help them to tune in to the world around us and become aware of how many issues affect children and how much advocacy for children is needed.

As you prepare for the first meeting of the group, you might also want to gather some related resources. See the endnotes and the bibliography. In the plans for each learning session, we also suggest a few resources that might be appropriate to the discussion generated by that session.

Introduction and Chapters 1–3

THIS SECTION OF THE BOOK is called "The Loom," as we see it as the framework for advocacy. It includes biblical and historical imperatives for caring and acting for children, discusses the theology of advocacy, and ends with a description of the contemporary world of children.

The Gathering

The purpose of the gathering time is to create community within your group and to set the stage for the discussion of this session.

Basic ideas for worship center: candle on a colored cloth (which would be used again each time you meet), the word *Advocate* in large print, some pictures of children of your community and the world.

As people arrive, greet them by name and welcome them. (Nametags may be helpful.) When all are gathered, light the candle as a sign of the beginning of the session. At this first session, discuss the worship center you have created, and encourage participants to bring items for the worship center.

Open with a prayer or responsive reading, such as: *Gracious and loving God, we gather today to better understand the children of our world, and to think about the many ways we can serve you as advocates for children. Bless our time together with your constant presence, help us listen to one another and help us make meaning of all that we experience in this time together. This we pray in the name of Jesus Christ, who loved children. Amen.*

Point to articles on your bulletin board of current events related to children, if you have chosen to do this (or create a website if you have those skills!). Continue to encourage people to look for and share related items in the news or from their daily lives.

Discussion and Response

Introduction and Chapter 1

Begin with a definition of advocacy. Our broadest definition is taking action on behalf of children. Look again at the introduction, and ask your group to define child advocacy out of their experiences. Discuss why they are a part of this study group, what brought them here and how advocacy has been a part of their lives.

Discuss the meaning of the word *theology*. In chapter 1, there are four important concepts describing the theology of advocacy:

1. The Nature of God
2. *Imago Dei*

3. Incarnation
4. Doctrine of Justice

Check with group members to see if they have questions about these concepts, and discuss. There may be questions that you and the group cannot answer. Don't be afraid to admit that, and remind people that searching for meaning is the common quest among you. You may wish to have group members research particular questions before the next meeting. Watch the clock! This discussion could be lengthy.

Look at the "Questions for Reflection" section at the end of chapter 1, and discuss the first question about understanding God's love.

Point to additional resources on the theology of child advocacy, particularly Eileen Lindner's book *Thus Far on the Way: Toward a Theology of Child Advocacy*.

Chapter 2

Divide the group into five groups, if possible. Assign each group one of the categories of Scripture readings listed in chapter 2: Biblical Mandates for Advocacy, Proscriptions against Harming Children, Inclusion of Children, Justice for Children, and Care for Children. Ask each group to read one or more of the Scripture readings in their category, and respond with a joint effort at drawing or sculpting of the main idea of that category. For example, for inclusion of children, one might draw open arms or a picture of Jesus and children. Share with the whole group.

—A short break might be helpful here—

After the break, quickly review "Biblical Images for Advocates" and the "Historical and Contemporary Images for Advocacy" in chapter 2. Discuss where participants found themselves in these stories and images. What characteristics of advocates from the Bible and history do we claim as our own? Depending on your group, respond to this discussion by asking participants to choose one of the characters listed and described how they are like/unlike them, *or* ask them which one they would most like to be and why. Remember that there are introverts and extroverts in every group. An extrovert will find this an easy task, but it might be very difficult for an introvert. Provide alternative ways to respond, perhaps in notebooks or journals instead of "out loud," and ask persons who wish to share to do so.

Chapter 3

Look at Diane's story about the playground she sees from her office. Does this correspond to your group's experience of today's children and culture? Make two lists as in a group discussion: What are the strengths or assets of families as they raise children in your community? What are the challenges to those families?

Then list ways the community is supporting families in response to both strengths and challenges. Specifically, are there ways the participants in your group (or your church) are working in these areas of challenge?

Describe your community through the categories list in chapter 3: socioeconomic, employment, support networks, schools, recreation. (Bring data with you to help with this discussion, such as census data or community reports.)

What are the varied cultural perspectives of your community, and what issues do these create? What strengths do they add?

If there have been major crises in your community, remember them at this time. Be aware that some people might be sensitive and grieving if crises are recent or extremely difficult. For example, if a large part of your community recently lost lives and homes in a weather-related crisis or accident, there may be some very vulnerable people in your group. You might begin this discussion with awareness that sensitivity and support are essential to the group's well-being.

Reflection and Closing

Ask the group to write down a comment about this meeting, something they learned and something they wonder about. Remind them of reading for the next session, about ways to share during the time they are apart (email lists? website?) Remind them to keep their eyes open for additions to your bulletin board and worship center.

Close with prayer, this one or one of your own choosing:

God of all people, we are grateful for this time together. We are grateful for the wisdom shared and the questions raised, but most of all, the call we hear to take action on behalf of children. Guide and support us, in Jesus' name, Amen.

Sending forth: **Go forth into the world to make a difference for children.**

Chapters 4–7

THESE CHAPTERS DISCUSS the different types of advocacy, the critical issues that have an impact on the lives of children and ways to "do" advocacy. When a weaver weaves, he or she first dresses the loom with the vertical threads called the warp, which creates the basic structure, the foundation, of the fabric. They are integral to the quality of the finished product.

The Gathering

Remember that the purpose of the gathering time is to create community within your group and to set the stage for discussion. Set up your worship center with the candle, cloth, and some of the articles you used in the last session, and add articles that might symbolize ideas from chapters 4–7. For example, chapter 4 begins with a story including chess, so you might bring a chess piece. Chapter 5 includes a summary of *Safe Sanctuaries*, so you might bring the book or resources related to it. Use your own creativity and find items meaningful to your group.

As people arrive, greet them by name and welcome them. When all are gathered, light the candle as a sign of the beginning of the session. Discuss the changes to the worship center you have created, and encourage sharing of items your participants may have brought to add to it.

Open with a prayer or responsive reading, such as: *Gracious and loving God, we gather again today to better understand the children of our world, and to think about the many ways we can serve you as advocates for children. Bless our time together with your constant presence, help us discern the places and issues of child advocacy in our world today, and to find ways we can begin to make changes that will make a difference. This we pray in the name of Jesus Christ, who loved children. Amen.*

Introduce your use of a bulletin board (or website) to post current events related to children if you have chosen to do this. Remind people to look for and share related items in the news or from their daily lives.

Discussion and Response

Given the many ideas for study generated by these chapters, if you have only an hour and a half for this session you will need to review and choose only four of the activities suggested below. In order to cover some of the main points of the chapters, choose at least one activity from each chapter.

Chapter 4

Read together or silently Mark 10:13–16. Discuss how your group (or your church or community) has welcomed children. Are the welcoming actions of your group solitary events or processes of acting on behalf of children over time?

Divide into four groups, each assigned with one of the four types of advocacy listed in chapter 4: education, service, public policy, and coalition building. (Use the worksheet, appendix D, "Planning Tool for Advocacy in the Local Church.") Ask each group to define the category and list examples out of their experiences. Have them report to the whole group on one example in your community of advocacy of the category they were assigned. Then, determine together whether the examples out of the groups are focused on groups of persons or are individually focused. Discuss their understandings of strategy in this context.

Chapter 5

Advocacy in the Church: Read the story together about the child who served First UMC as an usher, and contrast it with the following story about the congregation's reaction to the "shushing" usher. What is your church's experience with inclusion of children in these ways? How is child advocacy an issue of inclusion? Is ageism an issue in your church?

Look at the section on SWOT analyses. Post around the room newsprint or large pieces of paper labeled with the words *Strengths*, *Weaknesses*, *Opportunities*, and *Threats*. Discuss the idea that strengths and weaknesses relate to internal conditions and opportunities and threats exist as external conditions. Both affect potential success of current and future advocacy efforts of a church or agency. Give participants markers and ask them to walk around the room adding their ideas of the conditions in the four categories in this setting.

After a few minutes (be watching your time, perhaps include a break during this walking around time, or invite people to take a short break when they have finished adding their thoughts to the postings), call the group together and quickly share all of the conditions listed on the four sheets. Ask the group in the light of this quick SWOT analysis, what plans for advocacy could it make in this setting? (If your group participants do not have a common "setting," generalize to another level such as community or state or conference. Explain that a "real" SWOT analysis can actually take months, but that even this very quick one was helpful in sorting out data and understanding community needs and priorities.

—short break if you haven't taken one—

After the break, discuss the concept of "Safe Sanctuaries." If you are a church-based group, determine if your group thinks your church is safe for children, discuss why you feel it is or isn't, and why safety is a child advocacy issue. Consider asking group members to work on increasing safety in your church.

Bring brochures or other materials from agencies and organizations that benefit children. Help the group list other organizations serving children in your community. If your group or church is not currently affiliated with a child-serving organization, discuss how it might be. If there is sufficient interest in your group, determine a task group who will follow through and investigate a partnership with such an organization.

Chapter 6

Divide into groups to read and discuss the issues of the families from the Midwest, South, Northeast, and West. Ask each group to list issues of these families. When the groups are finished, post the lists on the same wall or lay them side by side on the table. What are the issues that confront children in every area of the country?

We say that poverty is the greatest threat to a child's well-being. Discuss whether or not the group feels that most of us accept child poverty, and how this is illustrated by contemporary life in this country.

At the end of the chapter, we strongly state that Jesus expects disciples to "touch the lives of children in pain with healing and hope" (page 109). Ask participants to respond to that statement by writing down one thing they can do to touch the lives of children with healing and hope. Respond to the statement by singing "Lord You Have Come to the Lakeshore" (*United Methodist Hymnal* 344) or a similar song or hymn that calls persons to service.

Chapter 7

Read Matthew 15:21–28 again, and discuss the advocacy efforts of the Canaanite woman. Ask the group how they think the woman felt through all of this—list emotions that may accompany advocacy efforts.

List the principles for effective advocacy. Discuss the content of each of these principles.

Seven steps are listed for organizing an advocacy program in a church or a group. Suggest a single issue-oriented program, such as eliminating child abuse, and ask the group to outline briefly the content of the seven steps for a campaign to eliminate child abuse. Just have them list one or two parts to each of the seven steps. It need not be complete or comprehensive since it will not be an actual program. Rather, it is a way to see that the group understands the steps required in the process of organizing a response program.

What does it mean to speak truth to power? What keeps advocates from speaking up? Make a list of characteristics of advocates that will empower them.

Reflection and Closing

Ask the group to write down a comment about this meeting, something they learned and something they wonder about. Remind them of reading for the next session, about ways to share during the time they are apart, and to continue to bring additions to your bulletin board and worship center.

Close with prayer, this one or one of your own choosing:

God of all people, we are grateful for this time together. We are grateful for the wisdom shared and the questions raised, but most of all, the call we hear to take action on behalf of children. Guide and support us, in Jesus' name. Amen.

Sending forth: **Go forth into the world to make a difference for children.**

Chapters 8–10

THE WEFT THREADS are woven into the fabric to complete it. These final chapters consider how individuals and churches can be involved in public-policy matters and our understanding of advocacy as vocation. We close with our hope for the realization of the *kindom* of God, the beloved community.

The Gathering

For the last time, we gather to create community within your group and to set the stage for the discussion of this session. Set up your worship center with the candle, cloth, and some of the articles you used in the last session, and add articles that might symbolize ideas from chapters 1–10. For example, you might include the quote from Micah, a picture of your state legislature, a wrapped gift. . . . There are many images in these chapters. Be creative and find items meaningful to your group.

As people arrive, greet them by name and welcome them. When all are gathered, light the candle as a sign of the beginning of the session. Discuss the changes to the worship center you have created, and encourage sharing of items your participants added.

Open with a prayer or responsive reading, such as: *Gracious and loving God, we gather again today to better understand the children of our world, and to think about the many ways we can serve you as advocates for children. Bless our time together with your constant presence, help us to understand ourselves and our vocations as child advocates. Guide us as we find ways we can begin to make changes for children of our community and world that will make a difference. This we pray in the name of Jesus Christ, who loved children. Amen.*

Post current events related to children, if you have chosen to do this. Ask people to share the items they have brought. Be prepared that there may be many more than your time can accommodate. It might be necessary to post the articles and review them later, or place the bulletin board in a public place where it can be shared.

Discussion and Response

Once again in consideration of the time available, you might find that it is necessary to choose one or two of the activities below.

Chapter 8

Look at Laura Dean's story about the press conference. Have any in your group had similar experiences, perhaps in a budget meeting at the church or in a parents meeting at the school?

Discuss how your denomination addresses public-policy issues. Which groups are making a difference in children's lives through their work?

There are three descriptions of churches out of the Protestants for the Common Good model. Which would best describe your church, and which would your group like your church to be? What are the barriers toward becoming that kind of church?

Take a few minutes and "do" a level 1 advocacy action. See appendixes E and F, "Worksheet for Writing Letters to Elected (Public) Officials" and "Communicating with Your Elected (Public) Officials." Ask the group how they can continue to do this kind of action in their church or group. Discuss how they might tackle a level 2 or 3 action.

Chapter 9

When has advocacy been difficult for persons in your group to do? In what ways do they feel disempowered by systems and by obstacles?

Discuss what discipleship means to the persons in your group? Ask each person to write his or her own definition, and discuss how these are like/unlike the definitions in this chapter. How is child advocacy discipleship? How is it stewardship?

What gifts does this group bring to child advocacy that might make a difference in the lives of children?

Chapter 10

This chapter is divided into three sections: Dream, Pray, and Work. Divide your group into three smaller groups and ask the three questions: For what do you dream? For what do you pray? and For what will you work? Ask the groups to respond in any way they wish—through a prayer, a plan for action, a description of the dream in a poem or song, or a dance. Share the responses in the whole group.

Reflection and Closing

Ask the group to fill out a short evaluation form for these sessions. Be sure to include positives (what they gained) as well as negatives (what prevented them from learning more or changes they would make).

Ask each person to write down one way she or he will assume the mantle of child advocacy this week. What specific actions will they take to make a difference in the lives of children? How can the group sustain the momentum they have experienced as a member of the study group? Is it time to begin a new children's council, an action team, a justice force?

Close with prayer, this or one of your own choosing:

God of all people, we are grateful for this time together. We are grateful for the wisdom shared and the questions raised, but most of all, for the call we hear to take action on behalf of children. We pray at this closing time for strength, persistence, and courage as we move into the world as child advocates. Guide and support us, in Jesus' name. Amen.

Sending forth: **Go forth into the world to make a difference for children.**

Note to facilitator: Be sure to summarize and file the evaluation comments with your notes from this study, so that next time you can use them. As a child advocate and a leader of such groups, this might be your way to change the world for children.

APPENDIX A

Bibliography

Allen, Susan and Julie Taylor. *Campaign for Children, Phase III: Public School Education*. New York: Women's Division, General Board of Global Ministries, The United Methodist Church, 2002. Hands-on guide for engaging United Methodist Women and local churches in advocacy for our communities' public schools. Includes practical strategies for supporting and improving schools. Available from Mission Resources, #3223, toll free 1-800-305-9857, fax 1-214-630-0079, www.missionresourcecenter.org.

Annie E. Casey Foundation. *Kids Count Data Book: State Profiles of Child Well-Being*. Baltimore, MD: Annie E. Casey Foundation. A national and state-by-state tracking of the status of children in the United States (published annually) to provide policymakers and citizens with benchmarks of child well-being in order to secure better futures for all children. Available from Annie E. Casey Foundation, 701 St. Paul Street, Baltimore, MD 21202, www.kidscount.org.

Children's Defense Fund. *Children's Sabbath Handbook*. Comprehensive reference published annually with specific themes for developing Children's Sabbath observances for faith communities and/or interfaith gatherings. Includes worship materials for Christian, Jewish, Muslim, and other faith traditions, lesson plans for education classes of all ages, and clip art for flyers and bulletins along with ideas for hands-on advocacy. Available from the

Children's Defense Fund. 25 E Street, NW, Washington, DC 20001, 202-628-8787, www.childrensdefense.org.

————. *Children's Topical Concordance of the Bible.* Developed by Shannon Daley-Harris, the concordance is organized in a series of topics related to the well-being of children, youth, and their families and God's call to work for justice on their behalf. This pocket-size New Revised Standard Version of the Bible also includes other typical references. Available from the Children's Defense Fund.

Crosson-Tower, Cynthia. *A Clergy Guide to Child Abuse and Neglect.* Cleveland, OH: The Pilgrim Press, 2006. Important presentation of explicit information about the issues of child abuse and domestic violence that places this information into the healing context of the church. Addresses how Christians must respond to and prevent child abuse and neglect and how clergy, especially, can care for themselves as well as their parishioners.

Couture, Pamela D. *Child Poverty: Love, Justice and Social Responsibility.* St. Louis: Chalice, 2007. Discussion of the variety of ways United Methodists minister with children who live in poverty using data gathered through interviews with conference leaders of the Bishops' Initiative on Children and Poverty. Calls for people of faith to see the faces of children in the most vexing social issues of our communities and our world.

————. *Seeing Children, Seeing God: A Practical Theology of Children and Poverty.* Nashville: Abingdon, 2000. Presentation of a practical pastoral framework for assessing and responding to the rights and well-being of children through weaving social, cultural, political, and ethical elements into a biblical theological model. Makes a compelling case for grace-filled and just care of children, particularly those who are vulnerable due to environment or circumstance.

Daly-Harris, Shannon, and Jeffrey Keenan, with Karen Speerstra. *Our Day to End Poverty: 24 Ways You Can Make a Difference.* San Francisco: Berrett-Koehler, 2007. Discussion of dozens of simple, often fun, and always practical actions you can take to help eliminate poverty in our day. Underscores the connections between our daily experiences and the suffering of people around the world. Available from the Children's Defense Fund.

Edelman, Marian Wright. *I'm Your Child, God: Prayers for Our Children.* City: Hyperion, 2002. Collection of prayers for children grouped by themes such as hope, love, and gratitude. Contains stunning collage artwork by award-winning illustrator, Bryan Collier. Available from the Children's Defense Fund.

Jenson, David H. *Graced Vulnerability: A Theology of Childhood.* Cleveland: Pilgrim, 2005. Provocative call to pay attention to children and to their lives, especially in consideration of the many threats to children's lives and well-being, such as war, poverty, abuse. Calls for the practice of vulnerability in the care of children, especially through the practices of the church.

Lindner, Eileen. *Thus Far on the Way: Toward a Theology of Child Advocacy.* edited by Shannon Daley-Harris (Louisville: Witherspoon, 2006). Collection of sermons delivered by Lindner at the Proctor Institute for Child Advocacy Ministry held annually at Haley Farm. Drawn from her experience of working for justice on behalf of all children, the book presents a compelling vision of advocacy ministry and communicates the urgency of immediate action for children. Available from Presbyterian Distribution Center, 100 Witherspoon Drive, Louisville, KY 40202, 1-800-524-2612, www.pcusa.org/marketplace.

May, Scottie, Beth Posterski, Catherine Stonehouse, and Linda Cannell. *Children Matter: Celebrating their Place in the Church, Family and Community.* Grand Rapids: Eerdmans, 2005. Contemporary discussion of the spirituality of children and the church's role in nurturing children. One of the distinguishing aspects of this book is the section on how adults can meet children's needs in worship, education, and in other specialized ministries.

Miller, Craig Kennet, and Mary Jane Pierce Norton. *Making God Real for a New Generation.* Nashville: Discipleship Resources, 2003. Thoughtful discussion about the generation of children born from 1982 to 1999, and their specific characteristics and needs. Contains sections on family life, the culture, spirituality, and models for ministry with this particular generation.

Melton, Joy Thornburg. *Safe Sanctuaries: Reducing the Risk of Abuse in the Church for Children and Youth.* Nashville: Discipleship Resources, 2008. Essential resources to guide congregations in the development of policies and procedures that reduce the risk of child abuse in the church. Book contains useful tools, worship materials, and training resources. Available from the Discipleship Resources, P.O. Box 340003, Nashville, TN 37203-0003, www.discipleshipresources.org.

Olson, Diane C. *Out of the Basement: A Holistic Approach to Children's Ministry.* Nashville, TN: Discipleship Resources, 2001. Helpful guide assists lay and clergy leaders in local congregations examine their children's ministry in a comprehensive and holistic manner. Covers a variety of systems within the church (e.g., pastoral care, education, space, safety, discipleship, mission, and advocacy). Available from Amazon.com.

Robinson, Adele, and Deborah R. Stark. *Advocates in Action: Making a Difference for Children*, rev. ed. Washington, DC: National Association for the Education of Young Children, 2005. Practical advice on influencing policy and practice to benefit young children and the early childhood community. Principles, strategies, and tools are applicable to other areas of child and youth concerns. Available from NAEYC, 1509 16th Street, NW, Washington, DC 20036-1426, 1-800-424-2460, www.naeyc.org.

The Task Force of the Bishops' Initiative on Children and Poverty. *Community with Children and the Poor: A Congregational Study.* Nashville: Cokesbury, 2003. Study resource includes seven sessions on Wesleyan heritage regarding children and the poor, impact of economic globalization, poverty in the United States and action planning to respond to the issues. Available from Cokesbury, #516543, 201 8th Avenue South, Nashville, TN 37202, 1-800-672-1789, www.cokesbury.com.

Yust, Karen Marie. *Real Kids, Real Faith: Practices for Nurturing Children's Spiritual Lives.* San Francisco: Jossey-Bass, 2004. Array of resources and tools needed by parents to guide and nurture their children in the development of a spiritual foundation for their lives. Particularly useful in helping parents identify their own important role in a child's deepening life of faith.

Important Advocacy Organizations

Annie E. Casey Foundation
701 St. Paul Street
Baltimore, MD 21202
www.aecf.org

Annie E. Casey Foundation conducts research and publishes its findings state by state on ten indicators of child well-being, including: low birth weight babies; infant mortality; child death rate; teen death rate; teen birth rate; teen dropout rate; teens not attending school or working; children living in families where no parent has full-time, year-round employment; number of children in poverty; and percent of children living in single-parent families. Their studies compare each state with national averages and also track the percentage of change over time. Annie E. Casey publishes *KIDS COUNT Data Book* on an annual basis. It is available at www.kidscount.org upon request at no charge.

Bread for the World
50 F Street, NW, Suite 500
Washington, DC 20001
www.bread.org

Bread for the World is a collective Christian voice urging our nation's decision makers to end hunger at home and abroad. Working in a bipartisan manner, Bread for the World encourages its members to communicate with their representatives in Congress through writing personal letters, emails, and face-to-face meetings. Every year, Bread for the World also invites churches across the country to participate in a nationwide Offering of Letters to Congress on an issue that is important to hungry people. Bread for the World collaborates with other organizations to build the political commitment needed to overcome hunger and poverty.

Children's Defense Fund
25 E. Street NW
Washington, DC 20001
www.childrensdefense.org

Children's Defense Fund (CDF) studies trends related to child well-being state by state, analyzes state and federal budgets and publishes statistics in several critical areas: education, child care, teen pregnancy and parenting, health, and poverty. CDF also coordinates the national observance of Children's Sabbath, usually held the third weekend of October so that people of faith will be thinking about children's issues when they go to the polls to vote in early November. See page 87 in chapter 5 for more information about Children's Sabbath. Order the Children's Sabbath guide annually at www.childrensdefense.org.

Every Child Matters Education Fund
2000 M Street NW, Suite 203
Washington, DC 20036
202-223-2000
www.everychildmatters.org

Every Child Matters Education Fund is a national nonprofit organization devoted to improving the lives of children and families by advocating for better public policy during federal and state campaigns. The organization focuses public attention on important children's issues including abuse and neglect, health care of low-income children, and early childhood care and education, after-school programs, and federal budget and tax issues. Its website includes a link to Project Vote Smart for voter registration and provides a media kit.

National Black Child Development Institute
1313 L Street, NW, #110
Washington, DC 20005-4110
202-833-2220
www.nbcdi.org

National Black Child Development Institute (NBCDI) educates the public about policy issues affecting African American children, produces timely research materials about black children, and convenes forums to discuss current issues facing the black community. Along with the affiliate network composed of volunteers from across the nation, NBCDI works to fulfill its mission to improve and protect the lives of children by strengthening child welfare services, making universal early care and education a reality, building family support services, pressing for educational reform, and providing vital information on children's health.

National Center for Children in Poverty
215 West 125th Street, 3rd floor
New York, NY 10027-4426
646-284-9600
www.nccp.org

National Center for Children in Poverty focuses its research and policy on the economic factors that contribute to child poverty. The Center outlines the difference between poverty and low income and generates fact sheets on low-income children in three age groupings—Birth to Age 3, Birth to Age 6, and Birth to Age 18—along with data on education, immigration, race, geography, mental health, and other factors. The site contains research studies on the economics of child and family issues and provides a link to the Child Care and Early Education Research Connection. The NCCP site also provides a monthly newsletter along with links to other sources of demographic data on children. www.nccp.org.

RESULTS
440 First Street NW, Suite 450
Washington, DC 20001
202-783-7100
www.results.org

RESULTS is an international citizens' lobby whose purpose is to create the political will to end hunger, at home and abroad, and to empower individuals in exercising their personal and political power. RESULTS identifies the most cost-effective programs that have a positive impact on the lives of the poor and then advocates for increased funding and replication of those programs. Composed of more than 800 grassroots volunteers in about 100 communities, RESULTS trains volunteers to speak powerfully to their elected officials, the media, and their local communities in order to inspire members of Congress to be leaders and spokespersons for the end of hunger and poverty.

UNICEF
333 East 38th Street, 6th floor
New York, NY 10016
www.unicef.org

UNICEF generates substantial data on a wide range of issues that affect children in the global community (i.e., poverty, hunger, education, child mortality, maternal health, HIV/AIDS, malaria and other diseases, abuse and neglect, and armed conflict). Its findings are published annually in *The State of the World's Children*.

Useful Advocacy Websites

Child Care Research
www.childcareresearch.org
Conduct research using this substantial collection of resources from many disciplines related to child care and early education, including early literacy, family child care, school-age child care, and professional development in early childhood, among others.

Federal Interagency Forum on Child and Family Statistics
www.childstats.gov
Review a report titled, *America's Children: Key National Indicators of Well-Being*, produced and posted annually. Visit this website or call the National Maternal Child Health Clearinghouse at 703-356-1964.

KIDS COUNT
www. kidscount/org
Use several interactive online databases that allow visitors to create free, customized data reports. The report choices vary by system, but include the ability to generate custom profiles, line graphs, maps, and rankings as well as to download raw data.

League of Women Voters
www.lwv.org
Register to vote at this website and obtain state-by-state information on voter eligibility requirements, registration deadlines, voting rights and responsibilities, and candidate profiles. It also lists the dates of all primaries and elections.

National Association for the Education of Young Children
www.naeyc.org
Find out about the Week of the Young Child, an annual celebration held each year in April to acknowledge the contribution of early childhood teachers and caregivers to the overall well-being of young children and to raise awareness of public policy issues that affect the lives of children of all ages and their parents.

National Center for Education Statistics
http://nces.ed.gov/
Gain online access to education databases and national statistics on education, updated on an annual basis in reports such as *The Condition of Education*. Call 202-502-2242.

National Child Care Information Center Child Care Database
www.nccic.org/IMS/Search.asp
Access information on child care in the United States, the District of Columbia, and Puerto Rico, in the following categories:

- Child Care and Development Fund
- Temporary Assistance to Needy Families (TANF)
- State Demographics
- Child Care Licensing
- Program Enrollment and Participation
- Professional Development

National Education Data Partnership
www.schoolmatters.com/
Study searchable information about public schools, school districts, and state education systems throughout the nation, including student achievement data, financial information, demographic breakdowns, tax base details, and more.

Prevent Child Abuse America
www.preventchildabuse.org
Locate child abuse statistics, current legislation, and methods for advocacy, including a detailed advocacy tool kit, the *Advocacy Guide*, which focuses specifically on advocacy efforts related to child abuse prevention. Principles,

strategies, and tools are applicable to a variety of other children and youth issues. Obtain the *Advocacy Guide* by contacting Prevent Child Abuse America, 200 South Michigan Avenue, 17th Floor, Chicago, IL 60604-2404, 312-663-3520, or by downloading the toolkit (200 pages) from the website.

United States Congress
www.house.gov
Find comprehensive information about the House of Representatives, including an organizational chart of the House, biographical directory of all Representatives, statistical information and committees and priorities of individual members of Congress. Use this site to identify the Representative for your Congressional district.

www.senate.gov
Gain comprehensive information about the Senate, including an organizational chart of the Senate, biographical directory of all senators, statistical information, and committees and priorities of individual senators. Use this site to identify the two senators from your state.

Voices for America's Children
www.voicesforamericaschildren.org
Learn about child advocacy through four major divisions found at this site: opportunities to make a difference, inspirational articles about advocates' successes, training for child advocates, and tools, including an electoral advocacy tool kit. Sign up for e-seminars Child Advocacy 101 and Federal Early Care and Education Policy and Funding, explore Voices' Nonprofit Management library, and stay up to date on public policy issues through the legislative e-brief.

APPENDIX D

Planning Tool

Building Effective Advocacy in the Local Church

Education

Explore issues, talk with parents, raise awareness of church and community

Identify (what we already do)

_____

_____

Plan (what we could do)

_____

_____

Act (how I will lead)

_____

_____

Service

Develop new programs, support existing programs, work as volunteer

Identify (what we already do)

_____

_____

Plan (what we could do)

_____

_____

Act (how I will lead)

_____

_____

Public Policy

Build relationships with legislators, advocate for or against specific legislation

Identify (what we already do)

_____

_____

Plan (what we could do)

_____

_____

Act (how I will lead)

_____

_____

Coalition Building

Organize group to address community problems, work in concert with others

Identify (what we already do)

_____

_____

Plan (what we could do)

_____

_____

Act (how I will lead)

_____

_____

Communicating with Your Legislators

Essentials

Be prepared. Be courteous. Be concise. Be passionate.

Methods

(In order of effectiveness)

Personal visits

- Begin cultivating a relationship with your legislators before the legislative session begins.
- Identify yourself as a person of faith and a constituent.
- Visit your legislators in their district offices—it's closer and usually less hectic there.
- Set up an appointment, whether you're going to the district office or the Capitol.
- Have two or three key points to share with your legislators. Take a fact sheet if you like.

Personal letters

- Begin with your legislator's full name, title, address, and salutation.
- Keep the body of your letters short. You can always attach an article or a fact sheet.
- Use your own words as much as possible. Form letters have limited impact.
- Include your address and phone number on your letter.
- Tell a story about a real-life experience you've had or you've observed.

Phone calls

- Call your legislator's office directly if urgent action is required on an issue.
- Talk with staff if you cannot speak directly with the legislator—staff can be helpful and influential.
- Organize your thoughts or write out two or three points that you want to make.
- Expect your call to last only two or three minutes.
- Practice what you will say before making the call.

E-mail messages or faxes

- Check with staff to be sure that your legislator reads e-mail messages.
- Write your message just as you would a letter (*see above*).
- Include your full name, address, and phone number at the bottom of your message.
- Send a fax if the matter is urgent or you prefer not to use e-mail.

Adapted from a flyer distributed by Nancy Amidei, Civic Engagement Project, University of Washington, Seattle, at a workshop, "Your Vote Counts," presented at the Quadrennial Conference for Community Ministries and Institutions, General Board of Global Ministries in Houston, November 13, 1999.